DATE DUE

★

The Federalist Era (1783–1800) is stamped in our history with special significance. Federalist leadership, under George Washington and Alexander Hamilton, drew up the Federal Constitution, won its ratification by the American people, and began the work of setting up a national government endowed with real, not just theoretical, power.

Bitter struggles went along with these achievements. The American people felt a deep distrust for government and its power to abuse them. Two great rebellions, Daniel Shays' in Massachusetts and the Whisky Rebellion in Pennsylvania, gave emphasis to the reality of their fears. The people insisted that the limits of Federal power be defined and set down imperishably in the Constitution. The Bill of Rights which they won set the guidelines for future struggles against oppressive rulers.

Another rift in American society was clear, but its depths had not yet been probed. In 1790 the future of 800,000 American slaves remained in doubt. But the continued existence of slavery underlined the fact that the Constitution was built upon compromise with the power and interests of slaveholders. Out of this, new struggles for human freedom would emerge.

The life or ordinary men and women, in those days, was hard and dangerous. The people lived constantly in the shadow of disease and death. The great Philadelphia Plague of 1793 was only one of the many epidemics that swept the countryside, wiping out families, filling the graveyards with new graves (many of them tiny) and leaving the air loud with the laments of the survivors.

Miss Starkey's eloquent pages bring to life the human conflicts of this stirring era.

LACE CUFFS AND LEATHER APRONS

The Living History Library
General Editor: John Anthony Scott

★

LACE CUFFS AND LEATHER APRONS

Popular Struggles in the Federalist Era

1783-1800

Marion Starkey

Illustrated with maps and contemporary prints

ALFRED A. KNOPF : NEW YORK

THIS IS A BORZOI BOOK PUBLISHED BY ALFRED A. KNOPF, INC.

Library of Congress Cataloging in Publication Data
Starkey, Marion Lena. Lace cuffs and leather aprons.

(The Living history library) SUMMARY: Examines the events that laid the foundation for the national government during the Federalist era that lasted from 1783 to 1803.

1. United States—History—Confederation, 1783–1789—Juvenile literature. 2. United States—History—Constitutional period, 1789–1809—Juvenile literature. [1. United States—History—Confederation, 1783–1789. 2. United States—History—Constitutional period, 1789–1809] I. Title E303.S8 973.4 75–113053 ISBN 0–394–82048–7 ISBN 0–394–92048–1 (lib. bdg.)

Manufactured in the United States of America
First Edition

Grateful acknowledgment is made for use of illustrations: American Antiquarian Society, 61; American Numismatic Society, 9, 76; Connecticut Historical Society, 153; Greenfield Village: Henry Ford Collections, 97; Henry Francis Dupont Winterthur Museum, 104, 240; Historical Society of Pennsylvania, 230; Library Company of Philadelphia, 37; National Gallery of Art, 30; New-York Historical Society, 27, 48, 70, 108, 111, 114, 124, 132, 143, 168, 169, 171, 185, 192, 205, 208, 252; New York Public Library, 15 (Prints Division), 19, 23, 51, 73, 81, 87, 159, 196 (Schomberg Collection), 218; Pennsylvania Hospital, 188; University of Virginia Library, 54. The maps in this book are by Edward Malsberg.

Grateful acknowledgment is made to The Shoe String Press, Inc. for permission to reprint from Eloise H. Linscott's Folk Songs of Old New England (Hamden, Ct.: Archon Books, 1962).

For Judy Engelhardt
*in grateful recognition of the enlivening of
these pages by the results of her research.*

CONTENTS

★

LACE CUFFS AND LEATHER APRONS

INTRODUCTION

This book tells the story of the Federalist era which lasted from the end of the Revolutionary War in 1783 to the election of Thomas Jefferson in 1801. In this period the foundations of national government were laid: the Constitution was written and ratified, the Bill of Rights was adopted, and a federal capital was established at Washington, D.C.

The United States was then made up of a population of about 4 million people, mostly very poor and very hard-working, who lived scattered about in a vast country that was to a large extent an uncleared wilderness. There were no railroads, no metaled roads for carriages, not more than a few bridges to span the streams that flowed from the western mountains to the Atlantic Ocean. The United States was a backward country, emerging slowly and painfully from a position of colonial dependency; even as African, Asian, and Latin American ex-colonies fight their way toward the sun today.

The country was torn by deep internal problems. Not a few people wondered if the American people would ever succeed as an independent nation. For example, on the question of slavery, Americans had proudly emblazoned on their revolutionary banner the ideal of human equality, the right to life, liberty, and the pursuit of happiness. But slavery did not die with the Revolution; by the end of the eighteenth century, there were over 800,000 slaves in the country, more slaves than there had ever been.

Thus slavery cast its own deep shadow over the Federalist era, molding the thinking of political leaders, the meaning of the Constitution, the very spirit of the Republic itself. Slavery was a grievous wound inflicted upon the young nation at its birth. It was, in the prophetic words of Tom Paine, "like a name engraved with the point of a pin on the tender rind of a young oak; the wound will enlarge with the tree, and posterity read it in full grown characters." The failure of the statesmanship of this era to tackle slavery and to eradicate it was something for which future generations of Americans, black and white alike, would pay dearly.

The American Constitution of 1787 reflected and expressed the divisions that existed in the American nation in yet another way. This document was composed of two parts: the draft drawn up in the Constitutional Convention at Philadelphia and the Bill of Rights which was added later.

The Bill of Rights was thrust into the Constitution at the insistence of a political opposition, the Anti-Federalists, who in this matter probably expressed the views of a majority of the people. Actually, the masses looked upon the idea of a central government with distrust. Had they not shed their blood in torrents to overthrow the rule of "the royal brute of England," George III? Did they not know that *all* government is evil, that a government in

Philadelphia or Washington would have as much capacity to do damage to ordinary people as a government in London—perhaps more?

Two major rebellions occurred in this period, Daniel Shays's Rebellion in Massachusetts, and the Whisky Rebellion in Pennsylvania. These movements underlined an important truth of the time, part of the heritage of this era to later days: ordinary men regarded government as at best a necessary evil, at worst a ruthless enemy. Liberty was something too important to be left to the protection of governments; it must be defended from day to day by the people themselves in the places where they lived, if necessary and in the last resort with arms in their hands.

★ 𝟏 ★

A YOUNG HEIR

The long war ended at last. Washington's ragged soldiers had finally triumphed over King George and the whole British Empire. But the mood of the veterans as they straggled home was seldom one of triumph.

Take young Elijah Fisher, for example. Fisher had been fighting for six years, then found himself a prisoner of war aboard a hellhole old ship, the *Jersey*. Released, he went looking for work but could find none. In December 1783 we find him making his way along the wharves of the waterfront at Boston. He was keeping a journal. "After I had been here inquiring and had ben on bord several of these Vessels," he wrote in it, "[I] could git into no bisiness neither by see nor Land." Disheartened, he returned to the center of Boston and sat down.

I com down by the market and sits down all alone allmost discouraged and begun to think over how that I had been in the army, what ill success I had met with there and allso how I was wronged by them I worked for at home, and lost all last winter, and now that I could not get into any business and no home.

Another veteran, Private Joseph Plumb Martin, ended

his war near West Point, New York. He wrote a book called A *Narrative of Some of the Adventures, Dangers, and Sufferings of a Revolutionary Soldier,* and in it often complained. He described his comrades on discharge— or, in his words, "when their fetters were knocked off"— as nearly threadbare. They had been promised coats, waistcoats, shirts, shoes and stockings, a pair of overalls and cap, and buckles and a blanket on enlisting. Of all that was promised, wrote Private Martin, they received "why perhaps a coat (we generally did get that) and one or two shirts . . . and all of the poorest quality, and blankets of thin baize, thin enough to have straws shot through them without discommoding the threads." He had further grievance:

How often have I had to lie whole stormy cold nights in a wood, on a field, or a bleak hill, with such blankets and other clothing like them, with nothing but the canopy of heaven to cover me. All this too in the heart of winter, when a New England farmer, if his cattle had been in my situation, would not have slept a wink from sheer anxiety for them. And if I stepped into a house to warm me, when passing, wet to the skin and almost dead with cold, hunger and fatigue, what scornful looks and hard words have I experienced.

The veterans set off for home as best they could; they had no travel allowance. But, for the moment, seeing how their womenfolk had managed the farm in their absence was all their interest. Hopefully they tried to cash their army pay certificates. This was virtually impossible; the certificates were largely worthless owing to the inflation, profiteering, and speculation that had set in during the latter days of the war. Numbers who had fought got no pay at all for months and years. Victory had amply repaid their patriotism. Nevertheless, wrote Private Martin,

We were promised six dollars and two thirds a month . . . and how did we fare in this particular? Why as we did in every other. I received the six dollars and two thirds till (if I remember rightly) the month of August 1777, when paying ceased.

And what was six dollars and sixty seven cents of this "Continental currency," as it was called, worth? It was scarcely enough to procure a man a dinner. Government was ashamed to tantalize the soldiers any longer with such trash, and wisely gave it up.

Martin had endured the bitter cold and near-starvation of Washington's winter quarters at Valley Forge, and a year later at Morristown, New Jersey. He could still feel his empty stomach:

Oftentimes I have gone one, two, three, and even four days without a morsel, unless the fields or forests might chance to afford enough to prevent absolute starvation. Often when I have picked the last grain from the bones of my scanty morsel, have I eat the very bones, as much of them as possibly could be eaten, and then have to perform some hard and fatiguing duty, when my stomach has been as craving as it was before I had eaten anything at all. . . .

When General Washington told Congress, "The sol-

Silver coin of the Confederation period showing an Indian princess on one side and a sun inscribed with thirteen stars on the other.

diers eat every kind of horse fodder but hay," he might have gone a little farther and told them that they eat considerable hog's fodder and not a trifle of dog's—when they could get it to eat.

Nevertheless, Private Martin was a young man who would land on his feet wherever they took him. Eventually he prospered in Maine, as did Private Fisher in spite of his early discouragement.

Katie Kruel

This colonial New England song was a favorite among veterans marching home from the Revolution.

When I first came to town They called me the rov - ing jew - el, Now they've changed their

tune, And call me Kat – ie Kru – el

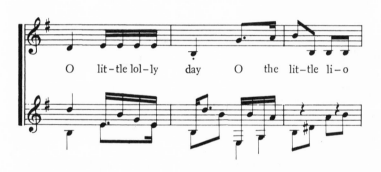

O lit –tle lol – ly day O the lit–tle li – o

REFRAIN

day. O that I were where I

2. I know who I love,
   And I know who does love me,
   I know where I'll go,
   And I know who'll go with me,
   O little lolly day,
   O the little lioday.

   O that I were where I would be,
   Then would I be where I am not,
   But I am where I must be,
   Where I would be I cannot,
   O little lolly day,
   O the little lioday.

3. Through the woods I'll go,
   And through the bog and mire,
   Straightway down the road
   Till I come to my heart's desire,
   O little lolly day,
   O the little lioday.

   O that I were where I would be,
   Then would I be where I am not,
   But I am where I must be,
   Where I would be I cannot,
   O little lolly day,
   O the little lioday.

Very little in either of these two accounts would have been a surprise to their commander, George Washington. Throughout the Revolution he had demanded of the Continental Congress, a working government hastily set up during the Revolution, better support of its fighting men, but his demands had mostly been in vain. As a result, some veterans who had got only a fraction of the face value of their certificates from speculators became so dissatisfied they made trouble. Eighty from the Pennsylvania militia marched on Congress and demanded their back pay. In Massachusetts, veterans were furious when the state would not accept their certificates in payment for taxes. One Massachusetts patriot became alarmed just listening to them: "You cannot hear them speak of the matter but in rage and flame. They are a fierce lot of men . . . when the collector is at the door demanding hard cash. . . . They burst out in a rage."

Writing to the governors of the thirteen states in 1783, Washington called attention not to these soldiers, but to the plight of his officers and disabled veterans. He deplored the melancholy and distressing sight of soldiers "who have shed their blood or lost their limbs in the service of the country, without a shelter, without a friend, and without the means of obtaining any of the necessaries or comforts of life, compelled to beg their daily bread from door to door." The Second Continental Congress had voted the disabled a pension for life, but Washington was dismally aware they were not likely to get it. This Congress could only ask for, not exact, funds from the states, and so was dependent on their convenience.

For many other Americans, too, having won a revolution was to bring a period of readjustment. Much of the countryside through which Martin and Fisher made their respective ways showed the havoc of war: houses ransacked, crops burned, stately groves leveled for firewood. The American people had fought the enemy on their home ground, an experience to be repeated on a limited scale in 1812, and far more extensively in the South during the Civil War.

The Alms House, Spruce Street, Philadelphia. Engraving by W. Birch,
1779.

It was, however, an unequal havoc. Massachusetts had suffered early, South Carolina late, Virginia early and late; Georgia and New Hampshire hardly knew there was a war going on. Some cities—Philadelphia, New York, Boston, and Providence, Rhode Island—had been occupied by hostile troops, some coastlines had been bombarded.

Meanwhile, travelers explored the country and made note of what war had done to it. Just a month after Washington composed his plea to the governors, a young German surgeon named Johann David Schoepf took advantage of the end of hostilities to tour the states. Schoepf had been in America since 1777, as an officer attached to a regiment of Hessians—the German mercenaries who had shipped to the colonies to fight alongside the British. But his stay had been mostly in Rhode Island and Manhattan, which he called "York Island." One result of his travels was the publication of a diary, *Travels in the Confederation 1783–84*, in which Schoepf appears as a man of not altogether democratic tastes, a keen and sometimes wry observer. His tour would take him to Philadelphia, to western Pennsylvania, back again to Philadelphia, then down the east coast. Being a scientist, his primary interests were botany and geology; yet he kept his eyes open and recorded what he saw of Americans after the Revolution.

Schoepf was shocked to see the low estate into which the Continental Congress had fallen, at least as evidenced by the newspapers. In Philadelphia, he wrote, "There are . . . every day lavished for the amusement of the public the bitterest mockeries over the high puissant

Congress, and nobody is held to account. The populace takes impudence to be liberty."

In part, it was the Congress's lack of power of the purse that had made it so weak and despised. While it had some powers, granted by the Articles of Confederation, an agreement drawn up between the thirteen states in 1777, the Continental Congress had no power to levy taxes. The states considered themselves most loosely united under the Articles, each state retaining its "sovereignty, freedom and independence"; they were but leagued together in "friendship with each other for their common defence, the security of their liberties, and their mutual and general welfare."

So, having exhausted its main source of funds, chiefly foreign loans from France and Holland, the Continental Congress had raised money by simply printing more of it. While this was done very respectably, there was an inevitable result:

The printing of money [Schoepf wrote] *was always done with a great circumspection; the paper was specially prepared and delineated; sworn persons were present and carefully counted off the sheets, and others signed each note with their names, and the blocks and letters were destroyed after every edition. . . .*

At first the bits of printed paper were to the people as valuable as hard coin. . . . Then a few merchants . . . began to ask for their wares the customary cash price, or double of it in paper money. . . . This device once adopted, the depreciation of paper money went forward irresistibly.

Long before the end of the war in 1783, the notes had become "dirty, decomposed, patched and unreadable . . . scarcely to be handled without contamination." Or, in the popular phrase, "not worth a continental."

What money there was in circulation was mostly shillings and pence left by the departing British, and some Spanish coin, silver dollars and pieces of eight. At first this supply was good; then it too was drawn off by hoarding and foreign trade. Soon, in order to make change, dollars were easily enough cut into halves and quarters. Some of these were called "sharp shins," after some sharp tradesmen who were not above cutting a silver dollar into five quarters. Similar practices, such as clipping both silver and gold, obliged American merchants to weigh every coin that came their way.

Some profiteering appeared to be going on, and one wonders if part of it was enriching the capital, then Philadelphia, as Schoepf found that city's citizens in fine fettle:

The war has left no sign of want here; now as before, the same exuberant plenty prevails. The inhabitants are not only well clothed but well fed, and, comparatively better than their betters in Europe. Few families can be found who do not enjoy daily their fine wheat-bread, good meats and fowls, cyder, beer, and rum.

Schoepf, incidentally, was delighted by Philadelphia's outdoor market where he found several curious dishes new to him: "raccoons, oppossums, fish-otters, bear bacon, and bear's foot &c. as well as many indigenous birds and fishes." Prices were not as low as before the war, but Schoepf was pleased to find he could still obtain a room

Philadelphia street scene from an engraving of the Federalist period.

in one of the public houses, with breakfast, dinner, and supper, for a few shillings a week.

On closer acquaintance, Philadelphians seemed to Schoepf to be suspicious of foreigners, so many of whom had recently been in their midst. But he saw that they hired French dancing masters, for the city was gay with concerts and balls, and the French had been sympathetic to the American cause. While before the war, "piano-fortes and such instruments were in the houses of the rich only as so much fashionable furniture . . . during the war and after it, straggling musicians from the various armies spread abroad a taste for music."

Throughout his travels Schoepf would make a point of visiting every state legislature he found in session. His comments, mostly unflattering, should perhaps be taken with a grain of salt, for he saw only what happened to take place on brief occasion, and the legislatures were operating under constitutions hastily improvised during the rebellion. Perhaps relatedly, they were also violating the Articles of Confederation: nine of them had navies (a power reserved to the Continental Congress), and four, like sovereign governments, were floating loans abroad. Virginia not only raised a private army to send into the interior on an unauthorized expedition to enlarge its boundaries, but blandly presented Congress with the bill.

Schoepf visited the Pennsylvania legislature several times. Nevertheless, as he reported,

I cannot say that in the strict sense I saw them sitting. At the upper end of the room the speaker or presi-

*dent of the assembly sits at a table in a rather high
chair. . . . The members sit in chairs at both sides of the
table . . . but seldom quietly, and in all manner of pos-
tures; some are going, some standing, and the greater part
seems pretty indifferent as to what is being said.*

When a vote was called at the assembly, it was customary for the yeas to rise, the nays to remain seated. A
fair proportion of the legislators were German country
folk, who had settled much of Pennsylvania. They
wore "blue stockings and yellow leather breeches" at-
tractive to Schoepf; many of them were not yet fluent
in English. So, he observed, they would usually sit tight
"until they see whether the greater number sits or stands,
and then they go the same so as to always keep with the
larger side." One man came up to Schoepf. "I wish they
had let me alone," he said. "What do I understand of
all that chitter? I wish I was home looking after my
things."

Leaving Philadelphia, Schoepf traveled leisurely west,
at night stopping to sleep at inns or in private homes
along the way. Near Valley Forge one evening, he
stopped at a Quaker house and engaged his hostess in
conversation.

*We lent the woman of the house a patient ear, and
received a circumstantial account of how her husband
during the war had, by a wise use of his post in the Land-
Office, got to himself a handsome estate, seven plantations, and could now laugh at the world. This he may do
with the more reason because he made his purchases
largely with paper-money, the no-value of which he per-*

ceived at the right time, using to his advantage the cre-
dulity of his patriotic fellow countrymen.

An innkeeper near Carlisle had turned to his own good
advantage the disarray of the Pennsylvania legislature. He

set up a saw-mill, and makes a profit on the boards, getting the logs for the mere trouble of taking them. For
these remote forests are at this time almost nobody's
property. With all the rest of the unsurveyed, unsold, or
unleased land, they were formerly the property of the
Penn family [notorious Tories], but now belong to the
state of Pennsylvania which has not the time to worry
over such a trifle as a few thousand tree-trunks.

The innkeeper also cleverly tanned hides, or so he said,
by rubbing them with the bark of chestnut oak.

Schoepf visited Wyoming Valley, twenty-six miles
of level land bordering the Susquehanna River. The inhabitants, who were technically citizens of Connecticut
though living in what is now Westmoreland County,
Pennsylvania, were "pauper-poor," he found. For them
"the war was something of a backset. . . . In the spring
they had neither seed-corn nor bread; lived meanwhile on
milk and blackberries, or by hunting (and many of them
on less), in expectation of the harvest."

Actually, though Schoepf was perhaps unaware of it,
Wyoming Valley had been the site of an ongoing border
dispute between the two states, Pennsylvania and Connecticut. A year after his visit, in fact, the Pennsylvania
militia evicted these settlers, as a letter from a man in
Wilkes-Barre testifies:

Hudson River saw mill, late 18th century.

[The soldiers] took away the garden fences, and have fenced in the town plot into large fields, and have forbid any inhabitants going into them on their own peril. Sentries are placed with such orders that no one dares to go into where their own gardens were. . . .

[The soldiers] forbid anyone hauling a seine to catch fish . . . so that people will fall short of their support which God and Nature allows them. . . .

The soldiers made a fence on the well-sweep that supplies most of the inhabitants near the fort with water, and swore that if anyone moved a rail of the fence the sentry would shoot them, which made some obliged to make use of the muddy water in the river. . . .

And their daily insults are beyond anything that could be believed.

The post-revolutionary period saw similar, if less violent disputes over boundaries erupt between Massachusetts and New York, between what called itself Vermont and New York and New Hampshire, and also in the South.

But Schoepf had moved on. At Fort Littleton he saw the specters of "cabins burnt during the war before the last," that is, the French and Indian wars. Other cabins had been abandoned in the more recent conflict, out of fear of the Crown's Indian allies. When Schoepf stopped at an inn in this desolate region, his host was full of suspicion: "He answered everything with No; one might ask for whiskey, cyder, milk, food, anything; he had in return for every question two others to put— Where bound? Where from? How far? Frenchmen? Prisoners? Looking for land? Trafficking? &c. &c."

Once one entered the foothills of the Allegheny Mountains, "roads" became delineated by broad axe-cuts in the trunks of trees. These shone white even at night, it was said. On one mountainside, the way had been barred by a landslide, but Schoepf got over by joining with

two heavily loaded wagons, carrying the baggage, women and children of several families traveling together. They lived far below the Ohio, on the Wabash; during the war they were taken captive by the Indians to Detroit, where they passed several years until the peace. . . . They travelled slowly and camped every night in the woods.

It was a romantic picture, and somewhat different from the charm of the city's balls, as perhaps Schoepf noted.

Anyway, he observed on his trip south shortly afterward, it was a plain fact that citizens of any one state seemed to consider even their next neighbors as foreigners. One might well ask, what did New Englanders tilling small subsistence farms really have in common with Georgians and Carolineans, wealthy gentleman-farmers? Or with the coastal people in New England, who were whalers and shipbuilders? Or with small merchants or bankers on "York Island"? Or with slaves? A New Englander had remarked, "I have never seen a Georgian."

It did seem plain to Schoepf that some Virginians he met near Smithfield (a region of pine forests renowned for its smoked hams, which Schoepf ungraciously referred to as "salted hog-meat") did not account themselves as having much in common with anybody. He listened as several gentleman-planters embroidered on *the great advantages which the Virginia state has over all other states in the world, and the nation of Virginia over all other nations. . . .*

Who in America [they asked] *would dare count himself the equal of the noble Virginian? The poor New Englander who gains his bread in the sweat of his brow? or the Pennsylvanian who drudges like a Negro and takes butter and cheese to market? or the North Carolina pitchboiler? or the South Carolinean with his everlasting rice? Above all there stands the Gentleman of Virginia, for he alone has the finest horses, the finest dogs, the most Negroes, the most land, speaks the best English, makes the most elegant bow, has the easy grace of a man of the world, and is a baron of his estates.*

Barons or not, Schoepf did not believe them when they claimed that during the Revolution no Virginian had been guilty of murder. But he let it go with a suppressed: "For the shooting done by their army in the high grass or creeping about in the bush on their stomachs so as to surprise and kill British soldiers, alone, unarmed and off their guard, they do not call murder." More bitterly: "They did not speak of the cases, not rare, of mulattoes out of Negresses by gentlemen who then sell their own children to others as slaves."

Touring, Schoepf found that Virginians had actually suffered more than they were willing to admit during the Revolution. At Yorktown, the scene of Cornwallis's surrender, "Several families were living in the ruins of buildings that had been shot to pieces." At Williamsburg: "I saw with concern the ravages of war wherever I went. . . . I heard no other subject but curses upon the English

Farming scene near Yorktown, Virginia, 1788.

government and armies." Schoepf himself suffered abuse; he was probably recognized as a Hessian whom the Americans had good cause to hate.

Yorktown was as near as Schoepf got to the Virginia coast. For the moment let us interrupt his narrative by the testimony of a young Englishman named Hadfield, who on landing in Norfolk was appalled by the devastation caused by what he called "the greatest revolution that ever happened." Before the war Norfolk had been a flourishing seaport. Now,

I saw nothing but ruins about me. Some people were repairing their houses and others living in sheds and outhouses. The only tavern . . . was wretched and crowded with a motley and noisy set of beings, many by their conduct and appearance half savage, nay worse than the Indian tribes. Englishmen were constantly liable to insult.

Schoepf arrived in Richmond to find the legislature in session. Here there were no fancy airs: "In the same clothes in which one goes hunting or tends his tobacco fields, it is permissable to appear in the senate or assembly. There are displayed boots, trousers, stockings and Indian leggings." Mr. Patrick Henry was there, evidently risen in the world for he had been "not so long ago . . . a country schoolmaster."

The Virginia statehouse, which Thomas Jefferson was to design on a classic pattern, had not yet been built. So the legislators sat in a small frame building, used also for balls and public banquets. Schoepf's observations were skeptical: "To judge from the indifference and heedlessness of most of their faces, it must be a trifling business to make laws. . . . In the anteroom there is a tumult . . . here they amuse themselves . . . with talk of horseraces, runaway Negroes, yesterday's play, politics."

The legislators were lodged in Richmond's one tavern, two stories, each containing a single room. On the second floor beds were arranged dormitory style, to the discomfort of Schoepf who liked privacy and in these travels seldom got it. On the first floor, "generals, colonels, captains, senators, assemblymen, judges, doctors, clerks . . . sat all together about the fire, drinking, smoking, singing and talking ribaldry." Outside stood their horses: "One could almost fancy it was an Arabian village; there were to be seen the whole day long saddled horses at every turn, and a swarming of riders in the few and muddy streets, for a horse must be mounted if only to fetch a prise of snuff from across the way."

Toward the end of 1783 Schoepf moved on to North Carolina. He found it warm even in wintertime. "Frogs were everywhere noisy in the swamps; bees flew; bats fluttered of an evening," he wrote. And the anecdotes were as colorful as the scenery. One he heard was about a man who

at a recent adjustment of the boundary line between Virginia and North Carolina . . . found that the line ran immediately behind the house . . . dividing his lands so that half lay in one state and half in the other. His dwelling-house stood on the Virginia side; and it occurred to him to build a new kitchen on the North Carolina side, so placed that the roof-tree should lie

Virginia hunting scene painted about 1800.

across the boundary. *He desired to have the pleasure of being able to say that he ate his meals every day in Virginia which had been prepared for him in North Carolina.*

This man was making pleasant amusement out of an unpleasant border arrangement between Virginia and North Carolina. Theoretically, as his wife left the kitchen she would have had to pay import duties, for Virginia was laying duties on what came and went across her borders. In retaliation, North Carolinians were considering setting up customs barriers of their own, but patrolling 150 miles of border or the complicated sea approaches was to prove beyond their power.

In February of the new year Schoepf visited Charleston, South Carolina, a city that charmed him so much that he rated it second only to Philadelphia. Oddly enough, the German, ordinarily a keen observer, thought Charleston already recovered from the havoc of war. (More than a decade later, a French traveler reported otherwise.) Schoepf recorded, though, a talk with a disgruntled major who told him

that during the whole of the war he had received no more than £70 in cash money, and that in order to live conformably to his position he had been obliged to sell many Negroes and even land at prices far below the real value.

For two and three years many officers had been paid not a bare shilling and the settlement of their claim by the state is as far off as ever. . . . They swear that neither they nor anyone else would ever be so foolish again as to

*dedicate themselves to the service of the state, fighting
for empty promises.*

The South Carolina legislature was in session and
Schoepf visited it. "The members from the city are for
the most part attorneys, considerable merchants . . .
intelligent and well informed," said our polite reporter;
"hence they are fluent, enterprising, and easily get the
upper hand of the representatives from the country."

The country faction, largely from the pine barrens,
seldom spoke but exercised their vote every time, thus
often surprising the other members. When the legislature voted to raise the tax on Negro slaves from one to
two dollars, for instance, country folk cared little. They
were not involved. But let the debate turn to whether
Tories guiltless of any crime but adherence to Great
Britain could return home, "with a veritably raging
obstinacy they breathed nothing but the bitterness of
vengeance, and could hear of no forgiveness. . . . The
blind zeal of the people was everywhere crying for
vengeance." Schoepf, used to European manners, ac-
corded his admiration to the city faction, whom he
described as "high-minded and estimable men [who]
used all their influence to recommend indulgence, forgiveness and gentle measures."

Was this "league of friendship" a nation or anything like it? With a bankrupt Congress and the squab-
bling between states the term had a hollow ring. Tories
still living in the states, or watching their chance to
return from exile in Canada or the West Indies,
smugly observed the signs of division, and looked to

see the Americans repent their rash bargain. Friends of the young nation, American patriots, watched with dismay, and none was more distressed than George Washington. Before his eyes the Continental Congress was crumbling into an undistinguished body with small talent for governing.

In the first excitement of the stand against Great Britain, the states had sent their best men to Congress. The signatures on the Declaration of Independence were a who's who of American talent. But as the war dragged on, as Congress failed to hold the states to their obligations in men and money, most of these leaders went home. They found more honor in serving on the home front than in a body rapidly declining in prestige. Those who replaced them were so lax in their duties that it was often impossible to get a quorum to carry on business. Washington, who had seen the war prolonged by governmental impotence, bitterly lamented

in the most poignant terms the fatal policy too prevalent in most of the states in employing their ablest men at home. . . . Where are our men of ability? Why do they not come forth to save their country?

Unless the states will content themselves with a full and well chosen representation in Congress, and vest that body with absolute powers in all matters relative to the great purposes of war . . . we shall soon become . . . a many-headed monster . . . that never will or can steer to the same point.

During the war Washington had often wondered if he commanded one army or thirteen. Somehow the "many-headed monster" had muddled through to peace. But could it win the peace? Were the states to go their separate ways? There was serious discussion that the practical arrangement would be for them to unite in three groups, New England, Middle, and Southern. But Washington would not give up his hope of a united nation.

I believe all things will come right at last, but like a young heir, come a little prematurely to a large inheritance, we shall wanton and run riot until we have brought our reputation to the brink of ruin, and then like him shall have to labor with the current of opinion, when compelled perhaps to do what prudence and common policy pointed out, as plain as any problem in Euclid. . . .

So said Washington in 1783, from Mount Vernon, where he hoped to live out his days as an obscure country gentleman.

★|2|★

A FLAWED FREEDOM

We resume with Dr. Schoepf passing through Virginia and North Carolina on his way to Charleston—to focus on a paradox not mentioned before. Riding overland Schoepf saw nothing of the great Virginia plantations, which habitually fronted on the water, and on the whole had an unflattering opinion of Virginians, of whose hospitality he saw little. Like Thomas Jefferson, he attributed their defects to slavery. "The introduction of the Negroes has been injurious to the moral principles of the inhabitants," he wrote, "has made them sluggish and arrogant, and at times cruel because of the despotic power they have over their slaves."

He reported an oddity he saw at Hanover courthouse:

On a very warm midday we found here a fine circle of ladies, silk-clad and tastefully coiffured, sitting about the fire. This was not so extraordinary in itself, but it was something new to me that several vigorous young blacks, quite naked, should be tumbling about before the party without giving scandal.

In Wilmington, North Carolina, he saw a slave auction. It included both outright sales of Negroes and

Negroes hired out for the year, the proceeds to go to their masters.

A cooper, indispensable in pitch and tar making, cost his purchaser £250, and his 15 year old boy, bred to the same work, fetched £150. The father was put up first; his anxiety lest his son fall to another purchaser and be separated from him was more painful than his fear of getting into the hands of a hard master. "Who buys me," he was continually calling out, "must buy my son too." It happened as he desired. But often the husband is snatched from his wife, the children from their mother. . . .

The auctioneer is at pains to enlarge upon the strength, beauty and health, capacity and sobriety of his wares, so as to obtain higher prices. On the other hand the Negroes zealously contradict everything good that is said about them, complain of their age, longstanding misery or sickness, and declare that the purchasers will be selling themselves in buying them . . . because they know well that the dearer their cost the more work will be required of them.

From Charleston Schoepf went to Nassau in the Bahamas, where it is a relief to read of a different situation.

Even the blacks here take part in the general contentment. They are everywhere of a better appearance, breathing happiness, strong, well-fed and of a decent appearance. Many of them are free, or if they are slaves, by paying a small weekly sum they are left undisturbed in the enjoyment of what they gain by other work. Some of

Allegorical painting by Samuel Jennings, 1790. It shows the figure of Liberty displaying the arts. The broken chain at her feet and the Black figures are meant to reveal the artist's keen sympathy with the abolitionist movement.

them own houses and plantations, and others are even put in command of small vessels.

"Breathing happiness." Would that ever describe the black people of America?

The most famous document of the Revolution had been the Declaration of Independence, drawn up to demonstrate "to a candid world" the case of the rebelling states against Great Britain. It did not have the force of law, it contained no plan of action, no rule of government; it was more compelling than law. Already people confused it with the Articles of Confederation. Later, when "the more perfect union" of which Washington dreamed, went into effect, people would mistake it for the Preamble to the Constitution.

It was often referred to as "Mr. Jefferson's declaration" in respect to its principal author. It was not, however, exactly as Mr. Jefferson had written it. The statement about inalienable rights had originally read "life, liberty, and property." The phrase "pursuit of happiness" had been substituted for property as more likely to appeal to the candid world.

More important had been the elimination of one major grievance against King George. Thomas Jefferson had expressed it thus:

He has waged cruel war against human nature itself, violating its most sacred rights of life and liberty in the persons of a distant people who never offended him, captivating and carrying them into slavery in another hemisphere, or to incur miserable death in their transportation hither.

This piratical warfare, the opprobrium of infidel powers is the warfare of the Christian king of Great Britain. Determined to keep open a market where MEN *should be bought and sold, he has [suppressed] every legislative attempt to prohibit or to restrain this execrable commerce; and that this assemblage of horrors might want no fact of distinguished die, he is now exciting those very people to rise in arms among us, and to purpose that liberty of which he deprived them, by murdering the people upon whom he also obtruded them; thus paying off former crimes against the liberties of one people, with crimes which he urges them to commit against the lives of another.*

The last sentence referred to the efforts of the last Royal Governor of Virginia, Lord Dunmore, to induce the slaves to desert their masters and come to him during the Revolution. He had been partly successful, and the resentment of Virginian masters demanded such expression as Jefferson had given it.

There was difficulty, however, with the statement with which this denunciation was linked. For the duration of the Revolution the southern states had been willing to put an end to the African slave trade. But what if circumstances changed? And how could they, whose economy, whose plantations of tobacco, rice, and indigo depended on slave labor, put their names to a statement which by implication denounced slavery itself? They could not and would not, and some northerners also refused.

The Two Sisters

This beautiful English ballad dates back hundreds of years. In Virginia, it was well-loved by both black and white people.

There lived an old lord by the north – ern sea,

Bow down; there lived an old lord by the north – ern sea, The

boughs they bend to me —— There lived an old lord by the

north – ern sea, And he had daught – ers

one, two, three. I will be true,

true to my love, love and my love will be

true to me. *Guitar break*

Verses 1-12. 2. A *Last verse*

2/ A young man came a-courting there,
   Bow down;
   A young man came a-courting there,
   The boughs they bend to me;
   A young man came a-courting there,
   He found the youngest very fair;
   I will be true, true to my love,
   Love, and my love will be true to me.

3/ He gave this girl a beaver hat,
   Bow down;
   He gave this girl a beaver hat,
   The boughs they bend to me;
   He gave this girl a beaver hat,
   The eldest she thought ill of that,
   I will be true, true to my love,
   Love, and my love will be true to me.

4/ He gave the youngest a gay gold ring,
   Bow down;
   He gave the youngest a gay gold ring,
   The boughs they bend to me;
   He gave the youngest a gay gold ring,
   But to the eldest not a thing,
   I will be true, true to my love,
   Love, and my love will be true to me.

5/ "Sister, oh sister, let us walk out,"
   Bow down;
   "Sister, oh sister, let us walk out,"
   The boughs they bend to me;
   "Sister, oh sister, let us walk out
   To see the ships go sailing about,"
   I will be true, true to my love,
   Love, and my love will be true to me.

6/ As they went a-walking at the sea's brim,
   Bow down;
   As they went a-walking at the sea's brim
   The boughs they bend to me,
   As they went-a-awalking at the sea's brim
   The eldest shoved the youngest in;
   I will be true, true to my love,
   Love and my love will be true to me.

7/ "Sister, oh sister, lend me your hand,"
   Bow down;
   "Sister, oh sister, lend me your hand,"
   The boughs they bend to me;
   "Sister, oh sister, lend me your hand,
   And you shall have my house and land,"
   I will be true, true to my love,
   Love, and my love will be true to me.

8/ "I'll give you neither hand nor glove,"
   Bow down;
   "I'll give you neither hand nor glove,"
   The boughs they bend to me;
   "I'll give you neither hand nor glove,
   But I will have your own true love,"
   I will be true, true to my love,
   Love and my love will be true to me.

9/ Down she sank and away she swam,
   Bow down;
   Down she sank and away she swam,
   The boughs they bend to me;
   Down she sank and away she swam,
   Until she came to the old mill dam;
   I will be true, true to my love,
   Love, and my love will be true to me.

10/ "Master, oh master, draw down your dam,"
Bow down;
"Master, oh master, draw down your dam,"
The boughs they bend to me;
"Master, oh master, draw down your dam,
There's either a mermaid or a swan,"
I will be true, true to my love,
Love, and my love will be true to me.

11/ The miller hastened and drew down the dam,
Bow down;
The miller hastened and drew down the dam,
The boughs they bend to me;
The miller hastened and drew down the dam,
And there he found a drowned woman,
I will be true, true to my love,
Love, and my love will be true to me.

12/ He cut off the finger with the gay gold ring,
Bow down;
He cut off the finger with the gay gold ring,
The boughs they bend to me;
He cut off the finger with the gay gold ring,
But to the girl's father he said not a thing,
I will be true, true to my love,
Love, and my love will be true to me.

13/ The miller was hanged at his own mill gate,
Bow down;
The miller was hanged at his own mill gate,
The boughs they bend to me,
The miller was hanged at his own mill gate,
The eldest sister she shared his fate,
I will be true, true to my love,
Love, and my love will be true to me.

It was not that slavery was either popular or profitable in the North. A movement for abolition had begun there in Puritan times, and was now being widely fostered by the Quakers. But if the North had small use for slave labor, its shipowners, especially in Rhode Island and Massachusetts, had profited enormously from the slave trade. What would be the reaction of the candid world if the new nation were presently to continue that which they had denounced King George for doing?

The embarrassing passage was struck out. But another, in the long run even more embarrassing, remained in the stirring second paragraph:

We hold these truths to be self-evident, that all men are created equal, that they are endowed by their Creator with certain unalienable Rights, that among these are Life, Liberty, and the pursuit of Happiness.—That to secure these rights, Governments are instituted among Men, deriving their just powers from the consent of the governed,—That whenever any Form of Government becomes destructive of these ends, it is the Right of the People to alter or abolish it, . . .

"Glittering generalities" some called the ringing phrases about equality and inalienable rights, for they were general compared to the honesty of the suppressed statement. Yet they impressed themselves on the hearts of many Americans, ringing out nearly as often as the chimes of Philadelphia's Christ Church. No Fourth of July oration was complete without them. In the South, though, masters had cause to be sensitive about letting their

Title page from Benjamin Bannaker's Almanac, 1795. Bannaker was a Black mathematician and surveyor. Although he had very little schooling, he made all his own weather predictions and astronomical calculations.

"people" (the well-bred seldom used the word *slave*) attend such celebrations. Too risky. Unlettered servants could not be expected to understand that they were not included in "all men." And as to ideas like liberty and "the consent of the governed" . . . Let them keep their distance and see what they could of the fireworks from the windows of the Big House.

Yet North and South there were those who worried about the contradiction between declaration and practice. Jefferson was one. In the waning days of the war, retired to his plantation Monticello in the hills of Charlottesville, he discussed the subject with a French friend for whom he was composing his *Notes on Virginia*.

Farseeing as he was, Jefferson was a man of his time, and as a slave-holding southerner he did not attribute equality to the Negro in "the endowments of body and mind." His experience with Negro intellect came from two sources, the astronomer Benjamin Bannaker, who had sent him an almanac of his own composition, and the poet Phillis Wheatley. He thought ill of the poems and unkindly suspected that the astronomer had been helped by a white man. But admitting the limitations of his experience, he showed some doubt of his judgment, and on the matter of justice he was eloquent.

First Jefferson deplored the effect of slavery on the master. He wrote:

The whole commerce between master and slave is a perpetual exercise of the most boisterous passions, the most unremitting despotism on the one part, and degrading submission on the other. Our children see this and learn to imitate it, for man is an imitative animal.

If a parent could find no motive, either in his phil-

anthropy or his self love, for restraining the intemper-
ance of passion towards his slave, it should always be a
sufficient one that his child is present. But generally it is
not sufficient. The parent storms, the child looks on,
catches the lineaments of wrath, puts on the same airs
in the circle of smaller slaves, gives a loose to the worst
of passions, and thus nursed, educated, and daily exercised in tyranny, cannot but be stamped by it. . . .

And can the liberties of a nation be thought secure
when we have removed their only firm basis—a conviction in the minds of the people that these liberties are
of the gift of God? That they are not to be violated but
with His wrath?

Indeed I tremble for my country when I remember
that God is just; that his justice cannot sleep forever;
that considering numbers, nature, and natural means only
a revolution of the wheel of fortune, an exchange of situation is among possible events; that it may become probable by supernatural interference! The Almighty has no
attribute which can take sides with us in such a contest.

What Jefferson then feared was a slave rebellion. Such
outbreaks had sometimes occurred in colonial times, and
would take place again. What he did not fear at the
time, but would live long enough to do so, was the con-
vulsion that would one day rend the states apart because
of slavery.

At the moment he had some hope:

I think a change already perceptible since the origin of
the present revolution. The spirit of the master is abating,
that of the slave rising from the dust, his condition mol-
lifying, the way—I hope—preparing under the auspices
of heaven for a total emancipation, and that this is dis-

Published according to Act of Parliament, Sept. 1, 1773 by Arch.ᵈ Bell.
Bookseller Nᵒ 8 near the Saracens Head Aldgate.

Famous 18th century Black poetess Phillis Wheatley; from the title page
of her Poems, published in 1773.

posed . . . to be with the consent of the masters rather than by their extirpation.

Jefferson looked for a change in the situation; he had also mentioned an "exchange of situation," an interesting prospect. Far less is known of him as a master than as a statesman, though he was for all intents and purposes a benevolent master. But he was a meticulous man, and kept a detailed diary of the affairs on his plantation in a small leatherbound notebook. And the *Memoirs* of one of his slaves, Isaac Smith or Isaac Jefferson as he called himself, adopting the master's surname as was the custom among slaves, have also been preserved, for Isaac Smith was interviewed in Richmond in 1847. Their accounts supplement each other, although it should be noted that Isaac Smith's *Memoirs* were written down in dialect, and perhaps edited by his interviewer. Jefferson's writing was, of course, his own.

Indeed, Jefferson was the owner of not one but seven plantations, comprising nearly 11,000 acres in four counties of Virginia's piedmont. Their names suggest tree-lined avenues, names such as Elk Hill, Shadwell, Lego, Cumberland, Tufton, and Poplar Forest. Monticello, the most beautiful, Jefferson designed himself over thirty careful years, and it still stands on a dome-shaped hill commanding a stunning view of the Charlottesville countryside.

Jefferson's *Farm Book*, entry to entry, tells about the weather one spring, the crops one fall, or how the brick kiln was doing on these seven plantations. In its pages are found axioms of farm husbandry, intelligent observations—for Jefferson may be said to have been the Leonardo of his time—about improving the construction of a portico or a lathe. A conservationist's mind is at work in the *Farm Book*. Every year Jefferson sowed several of his fields in flowering clover, which did not deplete the soil as did Virginia's big money crop, tobacco. The fields lay fallow. This was a practice George Washington observed too.

Numerous other pages of the *Farm Book* are devoted to the first names, activities, births, deaths of 187 Negro slaves, whom Jefferson had, incidentally, inherited. He thus soothed his conscience for not emancipating them, as some Virginians were doing. He did not believe there was any place for Negroes as free men in the society of his day, and indeed he was right in thinking so. Instead, he was carefully keeping track of the fields they planted, reaped, and harrowed; which of them cut the firewood; which slaves—often a phalanx of them—planted the corn at Lego plantation or grubbed the orchard for bugs at Elk Hill. The master had sometimes to copy out over a hundred names ("John Davy Lewis Johnny Isaac"), noting maternity ("Ursula's") and year of birth.

Isaac Smith had been born in 1775 to Ursula. The first hint of his existence in the *Farm Book* is this notation by Jefferson, for the year 1773: "Jan. 21. bot Ursula, and her sons George and Bagwell of Fleming's estate for £210. 12. months credit." Bagwell, at this time fourteen years old, and George, five years old—whom the *Farm Book* calls "George Smith"—had been bought with their mother. A year later, Ursula's third child, Archy, died: "Deaths 1774. Archy. Ursula's child. July." The cause of his death was not given, but a few pages on we come to

Isaac Jefferson, from an original photograph made about 1840.

a birth: "Births 1775. Isaac. (Ursula's. Monticello.) Dec."

Isaac Smith's account of himself is less succinct. One also wonders if he spoke in the third person, as the following seems to suggest, or if that was a device of the interviewer's:

Isaac Jefferson was born at Monticello. His mother was named Usler but nicknamed "Queen," because her husband was named George and commonly called "King George." She was pastry cook and washerwoman, stayed in the laundry. Isaac toted wood for her, made fire, and so on. Mrs. Jefferson would come out there with a cookery book in her hand and read out of it to Isaac's mother how to make cakes, tarts, and so on.

Perhaps his father was called King George only by the other slaves, for he was not strictly a field hand, but was a blacksmith, nailmaker, first manager of the Monticello nailery, and just before the turn of the nineteenth century, overseer at Monticello, a role usually reserved for whites. However, the *Farm Book* refers to him consistently as "Great George."

As boys, Isaac, George Smith, and Bagwell had their labor cut out for them, or if not labor at once—as Jefferson was not a hard master—at least their activities. The *Farm Book* advises· "Children till 10 years old to serve as nurses. From 10 to 16 the boys make nails, the girls spin. At 16 go into the ground or learn trades."

Isaac's brother Bagwell, sixteen by the time Isaac was born, was about ready to "go into the ground." His name begins to turn up in the *Farm Book* as one who stacked harvests at Lego, cradled wheat at Monticello. Isaac Smith went into trades. Between the ages of ten and sixteen he was tinsmithing and making nails. This was done within one of several "shops" Jefferson had built in a long row behind Monticello, about 200 feet downhill. Here were carried on home industries. There were a joiner's shop, blacksmith's shop, nail shop, spinning shop, and brick kiln. Slave-operated, these industries reflected Jefferson's idealistic hope that one day Americans, unlike their "betters" in Europe, would be a simple race of self-sustaining farmers, supplying most of their wants from the products of their own skills.

In this same row was slave housing; in the middle, an outhouse; at the end, a stable. The slave quarters were wooden, and Jefferson described them as "Servants houses of wood with wooden chimneys, & earth floors 12 x 14 feet each and 27 feet apart from each other." He had had them built close together, he wrote, that "fewer nurses may serve" while the parents were in the fields, "& that the children may be more easily attended by the superannuated women." Here Isaac Smith no doubt lived. He remembered,

Wolves so plenty that they had to build pens round the black people's quarters and pen sheep in 'em to keep the wolves from catching them. But they killed five or six of a night in the winter season; come and steal in the pens at night. When the snow was on the groun', you could see wolves in gangs runnin' and howlin.'

Isaac's description of a deer park at Monticello, which he and his father sometimes tended, was equally vivid.

The park was two or three miles round and fenced in with a high fence, twelve rails double-staked and ridered. . . . Isaac and his father fed the deer at sunup and sundown; called 'em up and fed 'em with corn. Had holes all along the fence at the feedin' place. Gave 'em salt; got right gentle; come up and eat out of your hand.

In 1780, when Isaac was five years old, the Virginia state government, operating in wartime emergency, moved from Williamsburg to Richmond. Jefferson was governor then, and took to Richmond with him Ursula, Isaac, and some other slaves, notably the "Hemingses." Isaac recalled that the latter were of mixed blood:

Bob Hemings drove the phaeton [carriage]; Jim Hemings was a body servant; Martin Hemings the butler. These three were brothers; Mary Hemings and Sally, their sister. Jim and Bob were bright mulattoes; Martin, darker. . . . Sally Hemings' mother was a bright mulatto woman and Sally mighty near white; she was the youngest child. Folks said that these Hemingses were old Mr. Wayles's [Jefferson's father-in-law] children.

All these people were in Richmond when British General Cornwallis's troops marched through Virginia in 1781 on the way to Yorktown, sacking plantations as they went along. Just after the Revolution, Jefferson recorded his damages from the British in the *Farm Book:*

Losses suffered the British in 1781.

2 blooded mares, 59 cattle, 30 sheep, 60 hogs, 200 barrels
corn in the house, 500 barrels corn growing and destroyed. . . . Hanibal, Polly, Sam, Sally, Nanny, Fanny,
Prince, Nancy fled to the enemy & died; Barnaby run
away, returned & died; Isabel Jack, Hannah's child,
Phoebe's child caught small pox and died. . . .

On a following page, the names of Great George, Ursula,
George Smith, Bagwell, and Isaac were listed as seized at
Richmond.

Isaac Smith himself remembered the coming of the
British into the city:

They formed a line, three cannon was heeled round all
at once and fired three rounds. Till they fired, the Richmond people thought they was a company come from
Petersburg to join them; some of 'em even hurrahed
when they seen them coming; but that moment they
knew it was the British. One of the cannonballs knocked
off the top of a butcher's house. The butcher's wife
screamed out and hollerd and her children too and all.
In ten minutes not a white man was to be seen in
Richmond.

Playing out-of-doors at the time, Isaac was brought in
by his mother. The British followed shortly, looking for
Jefferson. They did not find him, but led his slaves away
with them. Isaac Smith marched behind the wagons on
foot to Yorktown, while on the way the red-coated men
teased him. They called him "Sambo"; fortunately, they
also gave him "fresh meat and wheat bread," which he
remembered so many years later.

Before that decisive battle, a smallpox epidemic ran through the British camp:

It was very sickly at York; great many colored people died there. . . . Wallis [Cornwallis] had a cave dug and was hid in there. There was tremendous firing and smoke— seemed like heaven and earth was come together. Every time the great guns fire Isaac jump up off the ground. Heard the wounded men hollerin'. When the smoke blew off you could see the dead men laying on the ground.

After the American victory at Yorktown General Washington, southern planter that he was, and also a good friend to Jefferson, "brought all Mr. Jefferson's folks . . . back to Richmond with him and sent word to Mr. Jefferson to send down to Richmond for his servants."

So Isaac was sent back to Monticello. He was then six years old, and recalled handsome carriages driving up at the advent of peace. He had seen Patrick Henry appear in a "coach and two," and Washington's French ally, the Marquis de Lafayette, had given him "a guinea." He seemed to have been impressed by the gracious and peaceful way of life at Monticello. Formalities were observed, company or not. To have seen what follows, Isaac Smith must have been living in the main house near his mother, Ursula, Mrs. Jefferson's cook: "The supper table at Monticello was never set with less than eight covers at dinner if nobody at table but himself. Had from eight to thirty-two covers for dinner. Plenty of wine, best old Antiqua rum and cider; very fond of wine and water."

Jefferson's attire had also been commented on; before and during the war, he wore "a red waistcoat of Virginia-spun cloth." Afterward, after a trip to France (Jefferson became ambassador in 1785), he wore

a great many clothes . . . a coat of blue cloth trimmed with gold lace; cloak trimmed so too. Dar say it weighed fifty pounds. Large buttons on the coat as big as half a dollar; cloth set in the button; edge shine like gold. In summer, he wore silk coat, pearl buttons.

Correspondingly, the *Farm Book* records the clothing, food, and other arrangements for the Negroes. In the distribution of such essential goods, Jefferson for 1795 and 1796 had dealt with Isaac, Ursula, Bagwell, George Smith, and Great George thus:

Clothes 1795	yds linen	¾ yds cotton	¾ yds wool	stock-ings	shoes	blankets	bed
George	8		8	1	1	1	
Ursula	8		8	1	1		
Smith Geo.	7		7	1	1		1
Isaac	7		7	1	1		
Bagwell	7		7	1		1	
Clothes 1796							
George	8	8		1	1	1	
Ursula	8	9		1	1	1	
Smith Geo.	7	7		1	1	1	
Isaac	7	7		1	1		

Very many of these things could be made economically enough. From the *Farm Book:* "A side of upper leather & a side of soal make 6 pr shoes; & take ½ lb.

Anthony Benezet, Quaker abolitionist, teaching Black children.

thread, so that a hide & 1 lb. thread shoe 6 negroes." Slave "linen" was not as we know it, but made out of "cotton warp and hemp filling." Thus the reason for the following calculation: "A hand can tend 3 acres of hemp a year; a hand will break 60 or 70 lb. a day, & even to 150 lb. Tolerable ground yields 500 lbs. to the acre."

Calculation was also necessary in the distribution of foodstuffs. The *Farm Book* has it: "Hogs (hams, shoulders, midlings): In the distribution 4 children count as one grown person; the spinning girls count at ½; the nail boys count as one. . . ." Following this log a little further, in one year eighty hogs were slaughtered at Monticello. Sixty were reserved for Monticello, while there were "10 for the negroes."

Such unfair division over a long period of time could have led to resentment, but it is striking how little of this Isaac Smith seems to have felt. The white way of doing things had penetrated even to his daydreams. Once, sleeping over in the schoolhouse, to tend fire for the "scholars," he had observed the view: "You can see mountains all round as far as the eye can reach; sometimes see it rainin' . . . and the sun shining over the tops of the clouds. Willis Mountain sometimes looking in the clouds like a great house with two chimneys to it."

As for Jefferson, insofar as he had been calculating for his slaves, sometimes he tended to let this way of thinking slip into his vocabulary. For example, one year he had made a new plan for how the wheat harvest was to be done. It was 1795. But in 1796, according to the new plan,

the whole machine would move in exact equilibrio no

part of the force could be lessened without retarding the whole, nor increased without a waste of force. This force would cut, bring in, & stack 54 acres a day, and complete my harvest of 320 acres in 6 days.

This "whole machine" referred to the wheat harvesters at Monticello in 1795, who had been as follows:

1 Great George with tools & a grindstone mounted in the single mule cart should be constantly employed in mending cradles & grinding scythes. . . .
18 cradlers should work constantly George Smith, John, Davy, Lewis, Johnny, Isaac, Peter, Patrick, Ned, Toby, James, Val, Bagwell, Caesar, Jerry, Tim & Philip
18 Binders of the women & abler boys
6 gatherers, to wit, 5 small boys & 1 larger for a foreman.
3 Leaders Moses Shepherd & Joe loading the carts successively
6 Stackers Squire [Isaac's firstborn son by Iris] Abram Shoemaker Phil Essex Goliah Austin
2 Cooks O.Betty & Fanny
4 Carters Tom Phill Frank Martin
———
58
8 would remain to keep the ploughs a going Rachel Mary Nanny Sally Thamer Iris Scilla Phyllis.

Closing out this harvest, Jefferson kept track of what tools the slaves returned to him. Like many masters, he was fearful of theft. It seems pitiful that Bagwell returned "1 hilling hoe, 1 weed hoe, 1 axe, 1 pr wedges," and Iris, "1 grub hoe."

On another page, with respect to theft, Jefferson had

a note pertaining to Martin Hemings, the butler: "Recd from the Forest 4 Doz 10. bott. of Jamaica rum (note I shall keep tally of these as we use them by making a mark in the margin in order to try the fidelity of Martin.)"

For the first few months of any year, slaves would dig earth for bricks, cut pine and hickory and make up cords of firewood, and haul dung for fertilizer in mule carts. Planting began in April, harvesting in middle and late summer, but in autumn they more quietly gathered fodder, picked apples and peaches, and dug potatoes.

Once in the *Farm Book*, among entries for spring, a member of Isaac's family was mentioned.

Diary 1796
Apr. 26 There has been a most extraordinary drought through the whole spring to this time. The seeds down for a long time past have not sprouted. Copious rains now fall for 36 hours, gentle at first, heavy at last.
May 1 The first blossom I see of red clover
    5 Begin to cut clover . . .
    6 Iris lays in with a boy Joyce.
    10 Begin to sow peas

However, only a year or so later Isaac Smith's family begins to disappear from the *Farm Book*. That is, in 1797 Isaac, Iris, Joyce, and Squire were leased or hired to other masters. In 1801 another small family, Bagwell's, was also leased (all but Ursula, twelve years old, named after her grandmother), to Mr. John H. Craven, a man "who rents my farms here & my negroes." The names of Great George and George Smith are written in, then scratched out for the year 1799. It is apparent that Great George died, for: "Roll of the negroes in the winter of

1798–99, George 30 d. Nov. 2 99." This left Ursula alone, slotted for "distribution of crocus beds 94, 97, 1800." A few weeks later Ursula, too, died, and her death was recorded with a notice similar to that of her husband.

The Cherry Tree Carol

A lovely medieval carol, this was especially popular in the Appalachian region and Virginia.

Lace Cuffs and Leather Aprons

When Joseph and Mary
Walked through the orchard green,
There were apples and cherries
So many to be seen.
There were apples and cherries
So many to be seen.

Now Mary said to Joseph,
So meek and so mild,
"Joseph, gather me some cherries,
For I am with child.
Joseph, gather me some cherries,
For I am with child."

Then Joseph flew in anger,
In anger flew he.
"Let the father of thy baby
Gather cherries for thee.
Let the father of thy baby
Gather cherries for thee."

Then the tree spoke unto Mary,
And it began to bow,
"Mary, gather some cherries,
From the uttermost bough.
Mary, gather some cherries
From the uttermost bough."

TO THE WEST

In addition to the *Farm Book,* Jefferson left history a finer treatise: a description of the birds, animals, rivers, mountains, Indian life, and more in the western territory of America, which had recently been won from the British. Before turning to Jefferson's description of this domain, some background may be helpful. For if American independence became assured when Cornwallis surrendered in October 1781, nearly two more years would pass before "His Britannic Majesty" recognized his former colonies as "the said United States . . . to be free, sovereign and independent."

During this time one important question hung fire. How much land would England surrender? British policy had been to limit settlement to the land east of the Alleghenies. Were the states to be so restricted, or were their colonial charters to be confirmed? The charter given Massachusetts in 1629 had granted a narrow band of land "from the Atlantic and Westerne Sea and Ocean on the Easte Parte, to the South Sea on the Weste Parte." The "South Sea" was then the name of the Pacific Ocean, so the Massachusetts claim could be said to extend from coast to coast. Was the young upstart nation actually to receive so much?

It was indeed, but not yet. Even if England had been disposed to such generosity, there was another obstacle: the Spanish controlled the Mississippi, which placed the western limit of the new nation at the river's eastern bank.

Thanks to the shrewdness and patience of the aging Benjamin Franklin, who led John Jay and John Adams in the negotiations with England, the new country eventually did get that much. Franklin had also hoped for Canada, and managed to get a considerable slice of it. The northwestern boundary was to be the source of the Mississippi, then supposed to be the Lake of the Woods, well to the north and west of the true source, and America profited by geographical ignorance.

One article of the treaty concerned British military posts. "His Britannic Majesty shall, with all convenient speed . . . withdraw all his armies, garrisons and fleets from the said United States." The speed His Majesty found convenient did not please the Americans. England held its garrisons at Oswego and Detroit for years, and travelers to the greatest marvel of America had to get permission from the British to see Niagara Falls.

The Crown's excuse was the Americans' failure to live up to their treaty obligations, to return property taken from British subjects and to pay "in sterling money all bona fide debts." Tory property had been only imperfectly restored (in South Carolina, one Englishman was lynched when he made his claim, though this was unusual), while debts remained largely unpaid. So the British were keeping their garrisons.

Nevertheless, the treaty gave America a lordly in-

Niagara Falls drawn by the Irish traveler Isaac Weld, 1796.

heritance. A friend wrote Jefferson, "When the states on the Eastern shores . . . shall have become populous, rich and luxurious, and ready to yield their liberties into the hands of a tyrant, the gods of the mountains will save us, for they will be stronger than the gods of the valleys."

But the territory posed practical problems. How was the inheritance to be distributed? Were settlers to move in pell-mell as squatters? Such had been the case in colonial times, in spite of English prohibition, especially in the western part of Virginia that was about to become Kentucky. Few settlers in this area had clear land titles. Or were the lands to be bought up and controlled by speculators, as had in effect happened in New York under both Dutch and English rule. Were the poor to be kept out by the rich?

One problem had been solved during the Revolution. Not all colonial charters had grants that extended from coast to coast. The states were divided into the haves and the have-nots, and the latter were jealous of the former's unfair advantages. As early as 1776 Maryland had declared that "such lands ought to be common stock to be parceled out at any time into convenient, free, and independent governments." It had refused to sign the Articles of Confederation until 1781, when Virginia, following the lead of Massachusetts and Connecticut, yielded some of its huge western holdings to the common store. When two years later Virginia ceded most of its claim north of the Ohio, the Continental Congress set to work organizing what was soon called the Northwest Territory, and achieved its finest act of statesmanship.

No one gave more enthusiastic attention to this undertaking than Jefferson. Reared in the foothills of the Alleghenies, his gaze had always been westward. When he had composed his *Notes on Virginia*, his account of Virginia's rivers had covered not only the James and Potomac, but the Ohio, Mississippi, and even the Missouri. He called the Alleghenies "the spine of the country." Indeed, Jefferson had a sense of the American mountains that was almost biblical. He noted that they were not solitary mountains scattered "confusedly" over the face of the country, but that they "flowed one behind another" in ridges both north and south. From his home in Monticello he speculated that

this earth has been created in time, that the mountains were formed first, that the rivers began to flow afterwards, that in this place, particularly, they have been dammed up by the Blue Ridge of Mountains, and have formed an ocean which filled the whole valley; that continuing to rise they have at length broken over . . . and have torn the mountain down from its summit to its base. The piles of rock on each hand, but particularly on the Shenandoah, the evident marks of their disrupture and avulsion from their beds by the most powerful agents of nature, corroborates the impression.

"Infinitude" was the word Jefferson used to describe the abundance of these western lands. He began with the littlest pebbles, citing stone "white, blue, brown, &c., fit for the chisel, good mill-stone, such also as stands the fire, and slate stone." He wrote that "amythysts have been frequent and crystals common"; meanwhile, a very little of the iron, copper, and black lead were already undergoing mining. Actually, most of it was untouched. He marveled at: "The coal at Pittsburgh . . . A bed of it at that place has been a-fire since the year 1765. Another

Joseph Campbell, a Scottish visitor, as he traveled through the American west during the early 1790s.

coal-hill on the Pike-run of Monongahela [a western river] has been a-fire ten years; yet it has burnt away about twenty yards only."

One can well imagine the great deal of care, and sympathy, that went into his long lists of the animals and other wildlife of the western territories. Today's Americans may be curious to know that the Mississippi abounded with

turtle of a peculiar kind, perch, trout, gar, pike, mullets, herrings, carp, spatula-fish of fifty pounds weight, buffalo fish, and sturgeon. Alligators or crocodiles have been seen as high up as the Acansas. It also abounds in herons, cranes, ducks, brant, geese, and swans.

The Ohio River was, in Jefferson's words, "the most beautiful river on earth, its current gentle, waters clear." On its banks grew "Wild pea, Wild oat, Scarlet strawberries, Dewberries, Cloudberries, Wild crabapples, Wild plums, Wild hops, Cherokee plums, Upright honeysuckle. . . ." And he listed more. Hovering in the air: "Blue wing teal, Darkest crested heron, Chattering plover, Wild pigeon, Turtle dove, Black cap flycatcher, Little brown flycatcher, Yellow-bellied woodpecker, Wild goose . . ." while other animals buried themselves in prairies or wandered in shadows to escape predators. To name a few animals Jefferson listed: "Elk, Caribou, Red deer, Fallow deer, Jaguar, Cougar, Polecat, Red mole, Hare, Red squirrel, Gray squirrel, Flying squirrel, Water-rat, Weasel, Otter, Mink, Sloth, Beaver, Badger, White Bear."

The evening sky beyond the mountains was said to be

darkened by wild pigeons. Jefferson wrote that, west of the mountains, the horizon opened up blue to an infinite distance; at evening, at Bullet's Lick, Big-bones, and the Blue Lick, elk, deer, and caribou congregated for salt.

Intricately connected with this chain of living being were tribes of Chickasaw, Ottawa, Huron, Shawnee, among others Jefferson mentioned. They played games, one game resembling modern lacrosse, somewhat like the English game of cricket; they hunted or raised corn; and they made what to Jefferson must have seemed "small" wars.

Even the Indians' marriage ceremonies—appropriately so, since they regarded the earth as their "mother"— had reference to nature. As one white trapper quoted the rite in his memoirs: "*Nocey, cunner kee darmissey kee darniss nee zargayyar kakhaygo O waterwardoossin cawween peccan weeteey gammat ottertassey memarjis nee mor.*" (Father, I love your daughter, will you give her to me, that the small roots of her heart may entangle with mine, so that the strongest wind that blows shall never separate them.)

Compared to this trapper, Jefferson could only be a beginning student of the North American Indian, but he did have a feeling for them. In war he had found them "honorable." He had also found them artistic, imaginative, and affectionate to their children, "indeed indulgent in the extreme." Their numbers, though, had been "decimated" by contact with whites. Jefferson wrote that this was especially true of the easternmost tribes: "Spiritous liquors, the small-pox, war, and an abridgement of territory to a people who principally lived on the spon-

*1795 medal showing George Washing-
ton and an Indian chief.*

taneous productions of nature, had committed terrible havoc of them."

For Jefferson, the plight of these tribes, and the possibility that slavery might be introduced into western territory, were the only dampers on an otherwise boundless hope. He trusted other Americans to do as he had done, "look down into the workhouse of nature, to see her clouds, hail, snow, rain, thunder, all fabricated at our feet, and the glorious sun rising as if out of distant water, just gilding the mountains and giving life to all nature."

Jefferson also longed to know what he called the "terra incognita" that lay between the Father of Waters (the Mississippi) and the Pacific. One day he would satisfy this longing. But first he applied himself to the immediate problem—suggestions for settling, governing, and naming the new territory. He proposed a division into ten new states, and in naming them combined his knowledge of Greek and Indian terms. The Continental Congress rejected that part of his plan, and so rescued schoolboys from the task of learning to spell Polypotamia, Assenisipia, and Metropotamia. But two names, Illinois and Michigan, were to remain.

In 1787 Congress adopted the Northwest Ordinance which was based in part upon Jefferson's plan. The Northwest Ordinance addressed itself to the territory that lay within the huge triangle bounded by the Mississippi, the Ohio, and the Great Lakes. This territory would be known from that time forward as "the old northwest," to distinguish it from the lands south of the Ohio River, which were called "the old southwest." Not

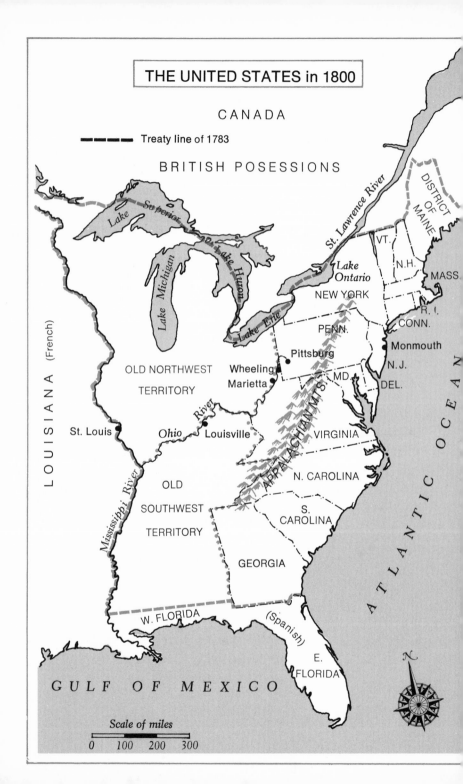

THE UNITED STATES in 1800

CANADA

▬ ▬ ▬ Treaty line of 1783

BRITISH POSESSIONS

Lake Superior

Lake Michigan

Lake Huron

St. Lawrence River

DISTRICT OF MAINE

VT.

N.H.

Lake Ontario

MASS.

NEW YORK

Lake Erie

R.I.

CONN.

PENN.

Pittsburg

Monmouth

N.J.

Wheeling

MD.

DEL.

Marietta

LOUISIANA (French)

OLD NORTHWEST TERRITORY

River

Ohio

Louisville

St. Louis

VIRGINIA

APPALACHIAN MTS.

Mississippi River

OLD SOUTHWEST TERRITORY

N. CAROLINA

S. CAROLINA

GEORGIA

ATLANTIC OCEAN

W. FLORIDA

(Spanish)

E. FLORIDA

GULF OF MEXICO

N

Scale of miles

0   100   200   300

less than three, nor more than five states were to be carved out of the old northwest. When in any part of the territory population reached 60,000, the people were at liberty to form a permanent constitution and state government, and to take their place with the other states in the Union "on an equal footing . . . in all respects whatever. . . ."

Also: "Religion, morality and knowledge being necessary to good government and the happiness of mankind, schools and the means of education shall be forever encouraged." An earlier ordinance in 1785 had provided the means: "There shall be reserved the lot No. 16 in every township for the maintenance of public schools."

One article of the Ordinance removed from the territory the great social flaw that worried Jefferson and shocked every visitor to the young nation: "There shall be neither slavery nor involuntary servitude in the said territory otherwise than in the punishment of crimes whereof the party shall have been duly convicted."

Indian rights were not forgotten:

The utmost good faith shall always be observed toward the Indians; their lands and property shall never be taken from them without their consent; and in their property rights and liberty they shall never be invaded or disturbed unless in just and lawful wars authorized by Congress; but laws founded in justice and humanity shall from time to time be made for preventing wrongs being done to them, and for peace and friendship with them.

This statement was wishful thinking and remained empty

rhetoric. When whites moved into Indian territory and the Indians resisted the stealing of their lands, they were mercilessly brushed aside in "unjust and unlawful wars."

The moment the Ordinance was passed, settlers began to pour westward. The town of Marietta in Ohio was among the earliest founded, and caravans could be seen going overland from the coast to Pittsburgh in wagons with big white letters on their coverings, "To Marietta on the Ohio." Enthusiastic letters from the territory drew more and more settlers. One said,

This country, for fertility of soil and pleasantness of situation, not only exceeds my expectations, but exceeds any part of America or Europe I ever was in. The climate is exceedingly healthy; not a man sick since we have been here. We have started 20 buffaloes in a drove. Deer are as plenty as sheep with you. Beaver and otter are abundant. I have known one man to catch 20 or 30 of them in two or three nights. Turkeys are innumerable; they come within a few rods of the fields. We have already planted a field of 150 acres in corn.

There were some dangers, especially to their livestock, from bears and panthers in the hills, and from wolves, as Isaac Smith had earlier mentioned.

To preserve their hogs [they] were obliged to build pens so high that the wolves could not jump or climb over them; or if in a low pen, covered with logs too heavy for them to remove. Large gangs of hogs in the woods would defend themselves by placing the young and feeble ones in the center of a ring formed by the old and stronger animals. If a wolf came within their reach, they

Marietta, pioneer settlement on the Ohio.

all fell upon him and tore him in pieces with their tusks and teeth.

Tall tales came back from some settlers, who "treated themselves to the jest respecting pumpkin vines that ran across the Ohio and bore pumpkins of a size to furnish space in which sows might litter." Such yarns, typical of the West, suggesting the Mark Twain of the future, produced equally tall tales from the East in response, as of "springs of brandy, flax that bore little pieces of cloth on the stems. . . . Accounts the most horrible were added of hoop snakes of such deadly malignity that a sting . . . when it punctured the bark of a green tree instantly caused its leaves to become sere and the tree to die."

Stories of Indian massacres and barbarities were related in all their horror, and Indian troubles there were, but nothing dampened the enthusiasm for settlement. In a very few years Ohio was dotted by villages which copied those left behind in New England, each with its village green and white meetinghouse. Not only were schools established as required by the Ordinance, but Marietta was planning a university. Later, such universities would house facsimiles of the more than a score of treaties, dating from this period to the early nineteenth century, by which the tribes relinquished their lands piecemeal, for coin or for hunting rights, lands they had regarded as their own.

We turn now to a lively account of journeying overland and downstream in the Northwest Territory, as recorded by Samuel E. Forman, who helped conduct a large party from New Jersey to the Mississippi at the end of November 1789. Forman was twenty-four at the time. Too young to have served with his brothers in the Revolution, this was the first major responsibility of his life, and its details were still vivid in his memory when he was persuaded to set them down half a century later, in *Narrative of a Journey Down the Ohio and Mississippi in 1789–90.*

The party included himself, his Uncle Forman's family (though not his uncle), Captain Benajah Osmun, and sixty slaves. Samuel wrote, "We had, I believe, four teams of four horses each, and one two-horse wagon, all covered with tow-cloth, while Captain Osmun and I rode on horseback."

General Forman, who would follow later—after a "distressing scene of taking leave—for the general's family and the blacks were almost all in tears"—had probably reasoned that, given the abolitionist trend in New Jersey (the Formans lived in Freehold), their state would not permit slavery indefinitely. Thus, although the party would pass through the Northwest Territory, where the Ordinance had forbidden slavery, they hoped to settle in what would later be southern Mississippi. They were the forerunners of many slaveowners moving from exhausted coastal acres to the more fertile west. Their practice would one day make a Midwest divided into slave and free territory, a source of dispute for the Civil War.

Samuel's descriptions of the blacks was:

There were 60 men, women, and children, and they were

the best set of blacks I ever saw together. I knew the most of them, and all were well behaved, except two rather ill-tempered fellows. General Forman purchased some more who had intermarried with his own, so as not to separate families. They were all well fed and well clothed.

Samuel described the first evening of their journey:

We encamped on the plains near Cranberry, having accomplished only 12 or 15 miles. The captain and I had a bed put under one of the wagons; the sides of the wagons had tenter-hooks, and curtains made to hook up to them, with loops to peg the bottom to the ground. The colored people mostly slept in their wagons.

In the night a heavy rain fell, when the captain and I fared badly. The ground was level, and the water, unable to run off, gave us a good soaking. I had on a new pair of handsome buckskins, small clothes.

Perhaps the buckskins helped at Lancaster, Pennsylvania, where the party was challenged by state authorities for transporting slaves west. Fortunately Samuel also had "all the necessary papers relating to the transportation of slaves through New Jersey and Pennsylvania." A Judge Hubley cleared them; afterward, one of the slave women came up to Samuel and informed him that the Lancaster ladies wanted some of the slaves to defect from the Forman party. She said that "the females of the city came out of their houses and inquired of them whether they could spin, knit, sew, and do housework, and whether they were willing to go to the South."

Sometimes it was lonely traveling in the western territory. One night, Samuel wrote,

The weather began to grow very cold, the roads bad and traveling tedious. We encamped . . . in the woods, kindled a fire, and turned the tails of the wagon all inward, thus forming a circle around the fire. . . . Another night we came to a vacant cabin without a floor; we made a large fire, and all who chose took their bedding and slept in the cabin, some remaining in the wagons.

Not long after, Forman ran into a brother's old army buddy, who risked the dignity of the strapping youth by giving him a bear hug and saying, "Why if this ain't little Sammy Forman." What was more welcome was his inviting the party to share all he had. "We remained till Monday, buying wheat and sending it to the mill, and converting a fat steer into meat, so that we were well provided for awhile."

The slave women's apparent willingness to go with the Formans from New Jersey into the Deep South was probably not shared by what Forman called the "two rather ill-tempered fellows," for now he briefly mentions an episode in Westmoreland County (where Schoepf had found people living on blackberries and hunting) where these two blacks were furnished with "old swords and pistols" by some free Negroes. Forman adds only, "but nothing serious grew out of it."

Then:

Somewhere about Fort Littleton or Fort Loudon, our

funds ran out. When we [had] left General Forman, he [had] told me that Uncle Ezekiel Forman would leave Philadelphia with his family, and overtake us in time to supply our wants. But he did not start as soon as he expected, and on his way into the mountains the top of his carriage got broken by a leaning tree, which somewhat detained him, so that we arrived at Pittsburgh two or three days before him._

Forman was trying to sell his horse in Pittsburgh to buy supplies when he met a storekeeper who knew his uncle Ezekiel. "Pointing to the large pile of silver dollars on the counter of the store, he said, 'Step up and help yourself to as much as you want and give me your [receipt].'" This was an unexpected favor. When the uncle arrived, he made good the loan.

The Pittsburgh Forman saw was a town of some 350 houses, with two weekly newspapers, and two shipyards to make boats for sailing downriver on the Ohio. These boats' keels were usually made of red, black, or white oak; masts were of pine. Perhaps rude by modern standards, Pittsburgh was a familiar embarking point for families, or large parties such as Forman's, setting out on the Ohio River with horses, cows, poultry, wagons, plows all on board. In the Formans' case,

It had taken us near three weeks to journey from Monmouth to Pittsburgh. After our arrival . . . our first business was to find situations for our numerous family, while awaiting the rise of the Ohio, and to lay in provisions for our long river voyage. Colonel Turnbull . . . an acquaintance of uncle [Ezekiel], politely offered him

Ohio river flat boat of the kind used to float merchandise downriver to New Orleans during the early national period.

the use of a vacant house and storeroom. . . . The colored people were all comfortably housed also.

The horses and wagons were sold at a great sacrifice—uncle [Ezekiel] retaining only his handsome coach horses and carriage, which he took to Natchez on a tobacco boat which Captain Osmun commanded, and on board of which the colored field hands were conveyed.

These [tobacco] boats were flat-bottomed and boarded over the top and appeared like floating houses. Uncle's boat was a 70 foot keel-boat, decked over, with a cabin for lodging purposes, but too low to stand up erect. The beds and bedding lay on the floor, and the insides lined with plank to prevent the Indians from penetrating through with their balls, should they attack us. We had a large quantity of dry goods, and a few were opened and bartered in payment for boats and provisions.

On board of the keel-boat, uncle and family found comfortable quarters. Mr. and Mrs. Forman, Augusta, Margaret, and Frances, aged about nine, eleven and thirteen; and David Forman, and the . . . housekeeper. I and five or six others, two mechanics, and about eight or ten house servants were also occupants of this boat.

The party left Pittsburgh on Sunday, after a friendly send-off.

Uncle Forman's keel-boat, Captain Osmun's flat-boat, and . . . a small keel-boat constituted our little fleet. The day of our departure was remarkably pleasant. Our number altogether must have reached very nearly a hundred. The dinner party accompanied us to our boats, and the wharf was covered with citizens. The river was very high and the current rapid. . . . Our keel-boat took the lead. These boats are guided by oars, seldom used, except the steering oar, or when passing islands, as the current goes about six or seven miles an hour. As the waters were now high, the current was perhaps eight or nine miles an hour.

On the banks of the Ohio they saw forests of sycamore, locust, birch, acacia, and red maple. Only every hundred miles or so might there be a cabin, and so Forman may not have seen even one on his second day's boat travel. Usually the cabins were without windows, occupied perhaps by a trapper and his wife, the latter sometimes an Indian; or perhaps by a settler family gaining their livelihood selling the pelts of stag and bear, cultivating Indian corn, peach trees. Usually only ten or twelve acres had been cleared, of several hundred owned.

The Banks of the Ohio

This well-known American song, known as a "murder ballad," originated in the early 19th century.

I asked my

Chorus:
And only say that you'll be mine,
In no other's arms entwine,
Down beside where the waters flow,
Down by the banks of the Ohio.

I held a knife against her breast,
As into my arms she pressed,
She cried, "Oh, Willie, don't murder me,
I'm not prepared for eternity."

Chorus

I started home between twelve and one,
I cried, "My God, what have I done?
Killed the only woman I loved
Because she would not be my bride."

Chorus

The party ran into the hazards of river navigation even before the second day.

Before daybreak . . . we made a narrow escape from destruction, from our ignorance of river navigation. The cable was made fast to small posts over the forecastle, where were fenders all around the little deck. When it began to grow dark, the anchor was thrown over, in hopes of holding us fast till morning, while the other boats were to tie up to trees along the river bank.

As soon as the anchor fastened itself in the river bottom, the boat gave a little lurch . . . the cable tore away all the framework around the deck, causing a great alarm. Several little black children were on deck at the time, and as it had now become quite dark, it could not be ascertained in the excitement of the moment, whether any of them had been thrown into the water. Fortunately none were missing.

During our confusion Captain Osmun's boat passed ours, a few minutes after the accident and [when] we passed him, he, hailing us, said that he was entangled in the top of a large tree, which had caved into the river, and requested the small rowboat to assist him. Uncle Forman immediately dispatched the two mechanics with the small boat to his assistance. Osmun got clear of the tree without injury, and the two mechanics rowed hard almost all night before they overtook him. . . .

After we lost our anchor, Uncle Forman took a chair and seated himself on the forecastle like a pilot, and I took the helm. He kept watch, notifying me when to change the direction of the boat. When he cried out to me "Port your helm," I was to keep straight in the middle of the stream; if to bear to the left he would cry out "Starboard"; if to the right, "Larboard."

Forman remarked that no one else could take the helm because no one else understood the terms; if his uncle really took starboard to mean left, it's no wonder.

I was not able to manage the helm alone, and had a man with me to assist in pulling as directed. . . . Ours was a perilous situation . . . it was the most distressing night I ever experienced.

The next morning [the third day out] all our boats landed at Wheeling, Virginia . . . 96 miles from Pittsburgh. Here we obtained a large steering oar for the keel-boats as the strong current kept the rudder from *acting without the application of great strength. Having adjusted matters, we set out again. We seldom ventured to land . . . for fear of lurking Indians.*

Before long they saw traces of them.

One day we discovered large flocks of wild turkeys flying about in the woods on shore. The blacksmith, who was a fine, active young man, asked Uncle Forman to set him on shore and give him a chance to kill some of them. The little boat was manned, and taking his rifle and a favorite dog, he soon landed.

But he had not been long on shore before he ran back to the river's bank, and made signs for the boat to come. . . . He said that he came to a large fire, and . . . supposed a party of Indians was not far off. He lost his fine dog, for he dared not call him.

They had one restful night in newly settled Marietta (Ohio), still "a dreary place," but enlivened by the singing of some young ladies. Three hundred miles downstream at Fort Washington, they spent two or three days enjoying the hospitality of the U.S. military garrison headed by General Harmar, commander of the troops for defense against the Indians in the Northwest Territory. At one dinner they were treated to "the haunch of a fine buffalo." Then,

The next morning after our entertainment by General Harmar and lady, we renewed our journey, floating rapidly down la Belle Rivière. Nothing of moment occurred till our arival at Louisville, at the Falls of the Ohio.

The weather now grew so severely cold, in the latter part of January, 1790, that the river became blocked with ice. Here we laid up, disembarked, and took a house in the village, the front part of which was furnished for a store. . . .

I opened a store from our stock of goods, and took tobacco in payment, which was the object in bringing the merchandise. Louisville then contained about 60 dwelling houses.

In Louisville, "It was the custom of the citizens, when any person of note arrived there, to get up a ball in their honor." Forman had the pleasure of attending one.

The ball was opened by a minuet by Uncle Forman and a southern lady—Aunt Forman did not dance. . . . Then two managers went around with numbers on paper in a hat—one going to the ladies, the other to the gentlemen. When the manager calls for lady No. 1, the lady drawing that number stands up and is led upon the floor, awaiting for gentleman No. 1. . . . I in my turn was drawn and introduced to my dancing partner from Maryland. . . . The officers of the garrison over the river generally attended and brought the military music along.

Forman probably also went skating, on numerous ponds behind Louisville; these in summer bred mosquitoes, in the wet season were stocked with fish. Tall chestnuts and oaks rose behind them, where perched wild turkeys, distinguishable from the domestic ones by their deep red feet.

By late February these ponds would still have been

frozen, but the river, according to Forman, was clear enough of ice for the fleet to continue. They left without him, for young Forman stayed behind to keep store. He was in painful suspense when he heard of Indian raids downstream. As he learned later, Uncle Ezekiel's party had indeed had a narrow escape.

A decoyer, who lived among the Indians, and whose business it was to lure boats ashore for the purposes of murder and robbery . . . saw the boats approaching, ran on the beach, imploring upon his bended knees that Mr. Forman, calling him by name, would come ashore and take him on board, as he had just escaped from the Indians.

Mr. Forman began to steer for his relief, when Captain Osmun, who was a little way in the rear, hailed Uncle, warning him to keep in the middle of the stream, as he saw Indians in hiding behind the trees along the bank, where the wily decoyer was playing his treacherous part.

It was an old trick, which had led several parties to their destruction.

The nephew, remaining in Louisville until he could sell off his stock, found that

The southern people are remarkably friendly to strangers. One family in particular, Mr. and Mrs. Ashby, were as kind to me as though I had been their own son. . . . Mrs. Ashby would come to my store like a mother, and inquire into the condition of my lodgings, sent bed and bedding, and had a kind old woman examine my trunk, taking out all my clothing, first airing and then nicely replacing them, and kindly did all my washing during my stay. . . .

Pioneer's quilt made in Connecticut about 1800.

I never parted with briefly made acquaintances with so much regret.

But first there were more dances. When Forman said he could not attend one because he had "no suitable pumps," a Virginia friend made a suggestion.

"You have purchased," said he, "a parcel of elegant moccasins for your New York ladies. You don one pair and I will another." . . . So we engaged our favorite partners and attended the ball. It was something new to appear in such an assembly decked off in such Indian gear; but they were much admired, and at the next dance almost all appeared in moccasins.

Occasional roughhouse centered around a local tavern. After one eggnog party all Forman's windows were broken. He got those responsible to pay for repairs, and what was perhaps more remarkable, introduced the town to the observance of the Sabbath.

It was observed one Sunday morning, soon after starting my store, that it was not opened on that day as other establishments were, and I was asked why I kept my store closed—that Sunday had not crossed the mountains, and I was the first person who kept his store shut on that day. I told them that I brought the Sabbath with me. It so happened that I had the honor of being the first to observe that day in Louisville.

Late in May, when a flotilla of tobacco boats stopped for repairs after making the falls of the Ohio, Forman took the opportunity to sell his store, buy a small tobacco boat, and descend the Ohio and Mississippi with the fleet. After troubles with navigation and a few Indian scares on the Ohio, he had his first look at the Mississippi.

When we arrived at the mouth of the Ohio we stopped. I fastened my boat to trees and the other boats did likewise. We kept watch with an ax in hand, to cut the fastenings in case of a surprise by Indians. Here were marks of buffalo having rested. Where the waters of the Mississippi and Ohio mingle, they look like putting dirty soap suds and pure water together. So we filled all our vessels that were water-tight for fear we might suffer for want of good water on our voyage. But we found out afterward that the Mississippi was very good water when filtered.

On the great river, where they ran into headwinds and daily thunderstorms "which made a heavy sea," they could no longer companionably lash some of their boats together or travel by night. But there was one big advantage. They were in Spanish territory, and Spain was at peace with the Indians, who need no longer be feared. One group even helped them row, and in return for refreshments aboard invited them to their camp, where unfortunately

some of our men must have let the Indians have la tafia, a cheap variety of rum distilled from molasses. They became very much intoxicated, and we were very apprehensive . . . but a squaw told us that the Indians could not fight, as she had secreted all their knives.

"Squaw" is not a word considered good form by Indians. Forman used it again when his party stopped at "Little Madrid," the American section of a Spanish garrison, and were detained several days by the lonely captain's insistent hospitality. Forman attended "a Spanish dance, all common people making up the company—French, Canadians, Spaniards, Americans. The belle of the ball was Cherokee Katy, a beautiful little squaw, dressed in Spanish style and decked off handsomely."

To the West

This melody is based on an old English song, *The Bonny Boy*.

down____ to the sea; Where a man is a man if he's

wil——ling to toil, And the humb-lest may gath–er the

fruits of the soil_____.

2/ Where children are blessings and he who have most
Has aid to his fortune and riches to boast,
Where the young maids exult and the aged may rest
Away far away in the land of the west

His journal may close here. It is perhaps a slight account of the everyday goings-on of the enthusiastic settlers who went to the territory for which Jefferson held so much hope. Looking at details, one wonders if Forman was the man to fulfill such hopes. Perhaps it is as well that when his time came for pioneering in earnest, he settled in tamer upper New York State. But actually, unless this be a tall tale, Forman had had a deed for several hundred acres of Northwest Territory land; the reason he gave for returning East, or one reason, was that his deed had been stolen from him. He did not say "stolen," but it had "disappeared mysteriously" from his trunk. Was it perhaps the kind old woman at Louisville? That *would* be a tall tale.

★ | 4 | ★

THE COMMOTIONS IN
MASSACHUSETTS

Events in America were watched across the Atlantic, sympathetically by the French, skeptically by the British. The latter confidently expected the new nation to fall apart, and in 1786 their view seemed justified. An editor of England's *Bath Chronicle* expressed his sentiments thus:

America exhibits a curious scene at this time, rebellion growing out of rebellion, particularly in that seeding bed and hotbed of discontent, sedition, riot and rebellion, Massachusetts Bay, where rebellion originates, breeds naturally, thrives and grows to maturity in the shortest time possible. There the doctrine of civil liberty, or every man his own government, has erected its standard and rides triumphantly over her embattled plains.

The term Massachusetts Bay, the name of Britain's former colony, and still used to some extent today, confused this English editor who had never seen it. Embattled or not, its plains were not extensive and hardly figured in the "discontent" of which he spoke. That had begun at Northampton in the shadow of Mount Tom; hilly Worcester followed suit, and the one pitched battle

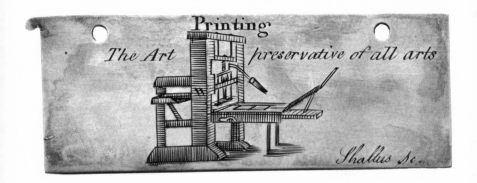

the discontent produced took place more than a hundred miles inland, in the Berkshires.

What was going on? Massachusetts farmers, mostly unpaid veterans of the Revolution, were rising against their state government. At first their activities were called "commotions"; later and reluctantly they were declared rebellion by the Bay State.

These events were more accurately reported in America. After the Revolution there were some 200 newspapers. Most were weeklies or semi-weeklies, printed on large sheets of rag paper; New York and Philadelphia had dailies.

Among the Massachusetts papers was the *Spy*, printed in Worcester by Isaiah Thomas. During the war Thomas had stayed awake nights turning out handbills and pamphlets against the British. His *Spy* was distributed free, thrice a week, from Salem Street at Boston; he had also printed broadsides for Boston's Sons of Liberty. At the advent of fighting he had to hurry his press away to Worcester, forty miles inland up the rugged Post Road, by night, and continued printing there in a cellar, helped by an apprentice, the way he had started out in the printing business at the age of seven.

By 1786, date of the "commotions," the *Spy*, still coming from Worcester, was no longer free but cost nine shillings and was run off on two presses. For a few years circulation had fluctuated; then it stabilized and shortly Thomas was to become one of the largest publishers on either side of the Atlantic. Nor was his prominence entirely due to the *Spy*, whose subscription circulation was at its peak, 1,200; in peacetime, Thomas was known as a printer of schoolbooks, ballads, farmer's almanacs, and classics. Once, apropos of a translation of Homer's *Iliad*, he performed a feat that few modern papers possess the type to duplicate: a passage of the English version and the Greek original in parallel columns. His paper had something for everyone, pieces written with formidable erudition side by side with accounts of rape reported down to the grimiest details. In 1786 he ordered from England a copy of the now-famous *Fanny Hill*, apparently intending to publish it. Under the pressure of events, however, he never did so. Thomas's printing office and countinghouse, painted yellow, were not far from the Worcester County Courthouse.

His publishing credo appeared in the issue of the *Spy* dated August 4, 1785:

The publisher of the Massachusetts Spy has ever been desirous of pleasing his readers. He thinks he has never neglected any means in his power to promote this purpose. He has been to great expense to enlarge this paper, and its present size exceeds any other printed in America. . . .

He requests the assistance of such of the Sons of Science as have leisure, to enable him to complete his plan, by furnishing him with such Essays as may be useful, improving or entertaining. He solicits the favour of the Reverend Clergy and others, in the several towns, whose desire is to do good, to oblige him with particular accounts of all useful discoveries, remarkable events, and all matters worthy of public attention which may occur within their knowledge.

One who responded to this advertisement in the early 1780s was not a son of science, but rather a Massachusetts farmer, and the testimonial he sent may be construed as a fable. It concerned this farmer's success and losses with six-rowed barley, "a species of barley that is very scarce." He had gotten four ears, he said, "by great luck and also expense," and

They were very green, and by keeping them very long in my pocket, the grain shriveled up to be very small; so that I was afraid they would not grow; being very dry, I steeped them in my pickle twenty-four hours, then as directed in this work, I candied or coated them over very well with the compound manure; and I believe every grain grew. Field mice would scratch to the grain, but leave it there.

Thus far, it escaped from waste, grew up and flourished greatly, each grain stooled or branched out from twenty to fifty ears, but just as it was shooting into ear, I had a mare tethered in the same [field], which broke loose, and cropped every root, which vexed me more than if the mare had died, which cost me thirty pounds; because I did not know where to get as much more, were I to give an hundred pound for it; however, contrary to my expectation, a great deal of it shot out, and grew a second time, but the forwardest ears which were shooting, grew no more; therefore I computed that about half my crop was lost by this mischance.

When it had gone into ear, what with people going to see it, and plucking it, and birds and mice feeding upon it, I lost a great deal more.

VENERATE THE PLOUGH

Engraving of a "happy ploughman" from the Columbian Magazine, 1787. Note the use of oxen, not horses, for ploughing.

The farmer optimistically concluded, "Notwithstanding all this I really believe I have two thousand fold for every grain I sowed."

Farmers frequently wrote the *Spy*, of such vicissitudes and successes. Many read it, and read as well *Thomas's Farmer's Almanack*, for which Thomas advertised in the *Spy* in October 1785.

Thomas's Almanack for 1786 is enlarged and improved, although at the usual price. It will contain two calendar pages for every month, one for Solar and one for Lunar calculations, on a new plan, easy to be understood. Besides the usual calculations of the Sun and Moon, Eclipses, &c. the Moon's age—the Length of days—the difference of time between the sun and clock—the moon's southing, &c. will be noted for every day in the year. To this will be added a concise Calendar for young Farmers and Gardeners, Showing the business of every month—the whole Bill of Rights of the inhabitants of Massachusetts. . . . Also, a list of the times and places of holding the court of Probate in the county of Worcester. The whole to contain forty-four pages of letter press.

One reason farmers would buy the *Almanack* had not to do with the moon's southing, but rather with dates and times of holding probate court (for distributing inheritances), and with its publication of the state's Bill of Rights, a section of the Massachusetts Constitution of 1780. Farmers were protesting their taxes at first in peaceable assembly. For Massachusetts, trying to pay off her war debt ($6.5 million) and share of the national war debt ($7.5 million) was taxing her citizens heavily. Heads of household living there in 1785 owed more taxes than their counterparts in 1900. The *Spy* regularly printed tax collectors' appointed arrivals.

What with heavy taxes and private creditors, many Massachusetts farmers were in debt, and were regularly hauled to court and sued. Here the farmer paid a lawyer's fee, and if he lost, a prosecuting attorney's fee as well as costs for writs and summonses, not written in Massachusetts in the 1780s without a fee. If a creditor won, a sheriff would seize oxen, grain, and farm, and auction them. Isaiah Thomas printed auction notices only rarely, but according to one that did appear, the debtor would lose in addition to everything else "Pew No. 9, in the Meeting-house."

Finally, the punishment for debt at this time was imprisonment, a too-harsh justice in 1785 when 94 of the 101 persons in jail in easterly Worcester were imprisoned for debt.

The farmers were suffering most severely in what had clearly become an economic depression in Massachusetts, perhaps because nervous creditors were not willing to accept pay in farm produce, an honored way of doing things in farm history. Massachusetts State would not accept this type of payment for taxes either, but Isaiah Thomas was good enough not to follow the state's example. He advertised in the *Spy:* "Indian corn, Flax Seed, or Beese Wax, will be received by the Printers of this Paper in payment from such persons as owe him, and have made the want of cash a plea for not paying him."

The *Spy*'s rider, who delivered the paper to outlying homes on horseback, was less charitable:

Edward Houghton HEREBY *gives notice to his Custom-*

JULY, Seventh Month, 1789.

LUNAR CALCULATIONS, &c.

● Full moon 7th day, 4th hour, morning.
☾ Laſt quarter 15th day, 4th hour, morning.
○ New moon 22d day, 11th hour, morning.
☽ Firſt quarter 29th day, 2d hour, morning.

M.D.	D.	Tides, Aſpects, Weather, &c.	● High Water A.	morn.	& eve.	pl.	● riſe &ſets.	● ſou. H.	M.
1	4	♄ ♃ Vc.	8	6 46	6 23	♏	0 9	7	31
2	5	Warm	9	7 33	7 10	♏	0 43	8	18
3	6	days	10	8 21	7 51	♏	1 18	9	7
4	7	and	11	9 21	8 51	♐	1 57	10	6
5	D	hot	12	10 15	9 45	♐	2 56	11	0
6	2	♀ ☿ ☌	13	11 5	10 35	♑	3 50	11	50
7	3	Middling Tides.	⊕	11 59	11 29	♒	☽ ſe.	morn.	
8	4	7*s riſe 0 h. 54 m.	15	morn.	E. 16	♒	7 57	0	44
9	5	nights,	16	0 36	1 5	♒	8 37	1	21
10	6	☍ ⊙°. ♋	17	1 33	2 2	♒	9 7	2	18
11	7	☽ Apogee.	18	2 18	2 47	♓	9 37	3	3
12	D	and	19	3 3	3 26	♓	9 53	3	48
13	2	☽ ♄ Vc.	20	3 42	4 12	♈	10 35	4	27
14	3	thunder	21	4 28	4 57	♈	10 52	5	13
15	4	ſhowers.	22	5 13	5 35	♈	11 39	5	58
16	5	Low Tides.	23	5 51	6 10	♉	11 57	6	36
17	6	Windy.	24	6 32	6 57	♉	morn.	7	17
18	7	♃ ♀ ☌	25	7 21	7 49	♊	0 26	8	6
19	D	Hot	26	8 13	8 41	♊	1 3	8	58
20	2	ſultry	27	9 5	9 40	♋	2 5	9	50
21	3	7*s riſe 11 h. 56 m.	28	10 4	10 39	♋	3 14	10	49
22	4	Weather.	○	11 5	11 40	♌	☽ ſets.	11	50
23	5	High Tides.	1	E. 18	morn.	♌	8 0	E.	50
24	6	♄ ☌ ſſ. ☽ Perig.	2	1 15	0 45	♍	8 38	1	50
25	7	Rain.	3	2 5	1 39	♍	9 6	2	50
26	D	Sultry	4	2 58	2 32	♎	9 39	3	43
27	2	Weather.	5	3 47	3 27	♎	10 8	4	32
28	3	☍ ⊙°. ♓	6	4 40	4 20	♎	10 45	5	25
29	4	Rain.	7	5 27	5 7	♏	11 16	6	12
30	5	Middling Tides.	8	6 23	5 55	♏	morn.	7	8
31	6	Warm.	9	7 9	6 41	♐	0 4	7	54

Page from Isaiah Thomas' Farmers Almanac, 1789.

ers, that he shall continue riding, as some of them have already settled for their papers, and he expects those who have not, to do it punctually at the close of the present quarter, which ends this week.

Those who neglect to settle their accounts this week may depend upon being sued, according to the promise made them last week.

This ad ran many times. Thomas also ran jail sentences, so it would be possible to see who was the next indebted farmer imprisoned, and how harsh justice was at the time. Often a debtor's fellow prisoner would have been a counterfeiter, or so we may guess from the following typical jail notices Thomas printed:

James Jewel was convicted of uttering and passing an counterfeit piece of money for a half johannes; and on another indightment for forging and uttering a counterfeit note of hand, he was sentenced to the pillory and whipping post, and to have one of his ears cropt [and to jail, from which he later escaped]. . . .

Glazier Wheeler, of Shutesbury, who has many years been famous for his adroitness in counterfeiting dollars, for coming fifty base dollars, was sent to stand in the pillory one hour, have his left ear cut off, be drawn from thence to the gallows, and set thereon with a rope about his neck for one hour, be publicly whipped on the naked back 20 stripes, committed to the house of correction without receiving the usual discipline thereof at the entrance, and kept there at hard labour for three years, and pay costs.

As a sidelight, another interesting sentence printed in

the *Spy* seems to have been the forerunner of *The Scarlet Letter* by Nathaniel Hawthorne:

Priscilla Wharfield, of Westfield, for adultery with a negro man, while her husband was in the army, to set one hour on the gallows with a rope about her neck, be severely whipped 20 stripes in the way from the gallows to the gaol, and forever after to wear a capital A two inches long, and of proportionable bigness, cut out in cloth of a contrary color to her clothes, sewed upon her upper garment on her back, in open view, and pay costs. . . .

The farmers' response to their taxes—as well as having their farms auctioned and then being imprisoned—was not a ruse, but protest. They had begun to hold mass gatherings, at which petitions were drawn up, and petitions for clemency addressed to the Massachusetts legislature (also called General Court), and to Governor James Bowdoin. Bowdoin was an intellectual, keenly interested in the experiments of Franklin, but had a vigorous respect for law and in Massachusetts was addressed as "His Excellency." The new *Worcester Magazine* printed a petition from citizens of Worcester County, drawn up by delegates from forty-one towns in September 1786. These petitioners begged leave to inform His Excellency Bowdoin and General Court that

The people in general are extremely embarrassed with public and private debts. No money can be obtained by the sale or mortgage of real estate; the produce of the present year, and the remainder of our cattle, even were

An American farming scene, Salisbury, Connecticut, 1789.

we to sell the whole, are totally inadequate to the present demands for money. Such has been our situation for some time past—an amazing flood of lawsuits has taken place—many industrious members of the community have been confined in gaol—and many more liable to the same calamity;—in a word, without relief, we have nothing before us but distress and ruin. In this deplorable condition, your petitioners humbly seek protection and redress from the wisdom of your Honours. . . .

The existence of the Courts of Common Pleas [for settlement of debtors' suits] and Court of General Session [for criminal cases], in their present mode of administration, has given general disgust to the good people of this county. These courts are an amazing expense to the subject, and in the opinion of your petitioners without the least conceivable advantage. . . . The feelings of the people are deeply wounded to see the officers of these courts living in the elegance of eastern magnificence, when at the same time they reflect that money is extracted by their distress.

The present practice of the law, and the exorbitancy of the fee table [money owed the legal profession] are universally complained of by the good people of this county, and we apprehend, not without reason. We think your honours will be of the same opinion if you turn your attention to the records of the clerk's office, the rules of the Bar, the insolence, influence, and increasing wealth of practitioners. . . .

We pray the Honorable Court for a prolongation of the time of the first payment of the present tax. . . .

We further pray that the Probate Courts may be so

regulated as to be more expeditious and decisive in their operations, and less grievous to the subject; as in the present mode many small estates are nearly swallowed up by the expenses, time and travel in attendance . . . therefore we pray your attention to every means proposed for the relief of debtors, as far as is consistent with the understanding of peace and national faith.

That the government made no satisfactory response to such an appeal was partly due to the petitioners' inadequate representation in the legislature. It was held against some of the towns most clamorous in their demands that they had sent no representative to the legislature. But they had sent none because they could not. Only a substantial property holder was eligible for such office, and in these hard times many villages could not find a single citizen who could qualify.

Instead of redressing the grievances, government officials saw to it that the newspapers set forth the state's case. Governor Bowdoin, in the *Worcester Magazine* for the second week in December, cautioned readers:

We feel in common with our neighbors the scarcity of money, but is not this scarcity owing to our own folly? At the close of the war, there was no complaint of it; since that time our fields have yielded their increase and heaven has showered its blessings on us in uncommon abundance; but are we not constrained to allow, that immense sums have been expended for what is of no value, for the gewgaws imported from Europe, and the more pernicious produce of the West-Indies [rum]. . . .

Without a reformation of manners, we can have little

hope to prosper in our publick or private concerns.

Really, the farmers thought, their government must be deaf. Petitioners from the town of Greenwich countered (as published in the *Worcester Magazine*):

Sirs, you say Let us lay aside the Destructive Fashions and expensive superfluities of the Day, be sober temperate &c., as becomes the younger to the Elder We thankfully acknowledge your good Counsel and beg leave to mention the good and old maxim Example is stronger than Precept. We pray you to consider what feeling the young and tender breast must be possest of when his own eyes sees his Elder Brother clothed in Purple and fine Lining and faring sumptuously every day and the younger obliged to submit to the Coursest fare and hard Toil clothed in Rags and yet belong to the same family.

Actually, some months before, events had gone further than petitions. Resistance, which Massachusetts was shortly to label "riots" and "rebellion," had occurred as early as August 1786. It began in the respectable and generally prosperous community of Northampton, a charming town with streets running parallel to the broad Connecticut River. On August 29 it was Northampton's turn to hold the Court of Common Pleas, for foreclosing on mortgages, confiscating debtors' goods, and sending delinquents to jail. That day farmers had poured down from the Berkshire hills to prevent the court from doing any of these things.

While some came with swords, guns, and cutlasses held from the Revolution, many had only wooden staves

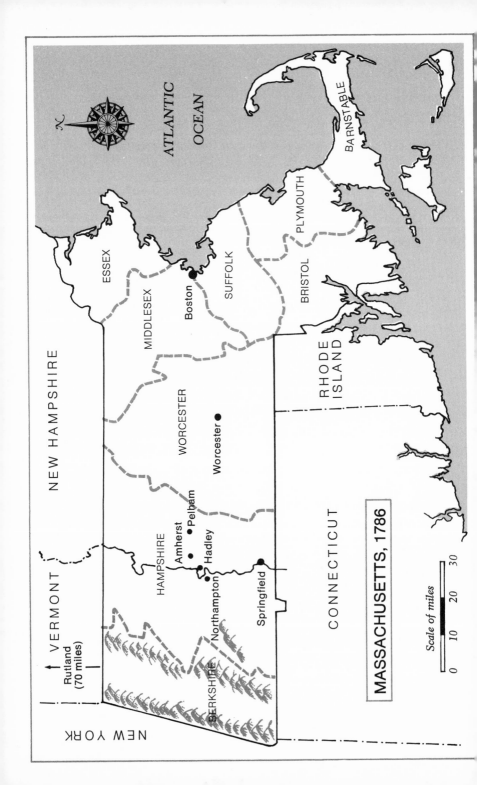

MASSACHUSETTS, 1786

in their hands. To keep their spirits up, they played fifes and drums, and appeared in town in early morning. By eleven o'clock they had amassed in such numbers—several hundred of them—that the sheriff at Northampton did not see how he could stop them. Calling on the state militia was futile. Much of it consisted of these militant farmers and the rest were sympathetic to the farmers' cause. Obviously, farmers intended to stop the court from sitting.

Against a background of quiet, well-kept homes where glass windows could be seen, and perhaps within fine china and silver plate, the farmers at fixed bayonet asked the silk-robed justices not to hold court. The justices kept an anxious eye on the crowd, and when by evening it had swelled to 1,500 people, they decided to oblige, and so adjourned. In the next few days similar mass gatherings stopped courts in Middlesex, Berkshire, and Bristol counties.

In the face of such a threat, the state legislature convened and a little progress was made. Some court fees were reduced. The Court of Common Pleas was suspended for several months, and arrangements were made to accept payment in kind for taxes. But the taxes were not reduced; the protests accordingly continued.

Farmers were by now being called "rebels," "insurgents," "Regulators," and "mob men." So banded together they found themselves a leader, although he was something of an unwilling one. He was Daniel Shays and he lived in a two-room house at Pelham, a farming village a few miles from Northampton, on the east side of the river. In the early years of the Revolution, after drilling boys armed with staves and broomsticks on Pelham's village green, Shays had fought gallantly at Bunker Hill, Saratoga, and Stony Point. More recently, he had not joined the crowds that stopped court in Northampton or elsewhere. His reason: "I told them it was inconsistent after they agreed to petition." But now, though Shays had never seen the inside of a debtor's prison, he too was in debt, in the same plight as his fellows, the other impoverished farmers and disillusioned veterans. So, a month after the "riots" at Northampton, he agreed to lead them, believing first and foremost that their grievances could be redressed without their having to resort to violence.

On September 25, 1786, farmers began descending on Springfield, twenty miles downriver from Northampton. They were in an especially angry mood. Regarding themselves as God-fearing but oppressed men, and by no means criminals, they had been astonished a few days before when Worcester Superior Court had indicted eleven of them as "disorderly, notorious and seditious persons [who] unlawfully and by force of arms [prevented] the due execution of justice and the law of the Commonwealth." The court at Springfield, a criminal court, was getting ready to rule on similar cases. Before it did, Daniel Shays prepared to deliver to it a petition requesting, or demanding, that "those currently in arms for the purpose of defending their persons and properties by preventing the court of Common Pleas" not be prosecuted as if they were criminals.

The sheriff at Springfield lost no time. On Monday, September 26, he called out the militia, and got a fair response. General William Shepard, who lived nearby, opened the arsenal in Springfield to help defend the court. Under his direction, field weapons were set up before the courthouse. Then the bewigged judges, and such of the jury as came, arrived armed with rifles.

As the day wore on, the temper of the crowd of farmers, constantly reinforced from the countryside, grew heated. Shays tried to work off their restlessness by parading them with the soldierly precision he had practiced during the Revolution. Some of them were still wearing Continental uniforms, now ragged, but most wore earth-stained work clothes. Shays asked each to wear, as a badge of loyalty, a sprig of hemlock in his cap. Then he dressed ranks smartly, and placed a nineteen-year-old Pelham boy, who had a first-rate horse and rode it with style, at the head of the ranks.

Against the protesters, the militia defending the court wore, as badges of their loyalty, bits of white paper. But as they watched Shays's ranks march and countermarch, the inevitable happened: some of the militia threw away their bits of white paper, went over to the other side, and put hemlock in their caps to march with Daniel Shays.

The whole affair lasted three days and the good citizens of Springfield, terrified, hardly dared leave their houses. In the end, the court did not sit, and Shays, unheard-of before, became "the celebrated Captain Shays." Editors dug up every bit of information they could find about him.

Shays had not considered his actions in Springfield subversive or treasonous. Had it not been done to keep order? "I am so far from considering it a crime," he told a friend, "that I look upon it that the government are indebted to me for what I did there."

The government thought otherwise. A long and significant notice was printed shortly afterward in the *Worcester Magazine*, no doubt with pleasure by printer Thomas, who no longer had any liking for "mob men."

RIOT ACT

In the year of Our Lord One Thousand Seven Hundred and Eighty-six. An Act to prevent Routs, Riots, and tumultuous Assemblies, and the evil consequences thereof:

Whereas the provision already made by law, for the prevention of Routs, Riots and tumultuous Assemblies, and the evil Consequences thereof, has been found insufficient:

Be it therefore Enacted by the Senate and House of Representatives in General Court assembled, and by the Authority of the same, That from and after the publication of this Act, if any persons to the number of twelve or more, Being armed with clubs or other weapons; or if any number of persons, consisting of thirty, or more, shall be unlawfully, riotously and tumultuously assembled, any Justice of the Peace, Sheriff, or Deputy-Sheriff of the court, or Constable of the Town, shall come among the Rioters, or as near to them as he can safely come, command silence . . . and shall openly make Proclamation in these or the like words:

Citizens of Massachusetts

By virtue of an act of this Commonwealth, made and passed in the year our Lord, one thousand seven hundred and eighty-six entitled, "An act for suppressing Routs,

Riots, and tumultuous Assemblies, and the evil consequences thereof," I am directed to charge and command, and I do accordingly charge and command, all persons, being here assembled, immediately to disperse themselves, and peaceably to depart to their habitations, or to their lawful business, upon the pains inflicted by said act. GOD save the COMMONWEALTH.

And if such persons, assembled as aforesaid, shall not disperse themselves within one hour after Proclamation made, or attempted to be made as aforesaid, it shall be lawful for every such officer to command sufficient aid and he shall seize such persons, who shall be had before a Justice of the Peace, Sheriff, or Deputy-Sheriff; [he] is hereby further empowered to require the aid of a sufficient number of persons in arms, if any of the persons, assembled as aforesaid, shall appear armed. And if any such person or persons shall be killed or wounded, by reason of his or their resisting the persons endeavoring to disperse or seize them, the said Justice, Sheriff, Deputy-Sheriff, Constable and their assistants, shall be indemnified and held guiltless.

AND be it further enacted, That all persons, who for the space of one hour after the proclamation made or attempted to be made, as aforesaid, shall unlawfully, riotously, and tumultuously continue together, or shall willfully let, or hinder any such officer, who shall be known, or shall openly declare himself to be such, from making the said proclamation, shall forfeit all their Lands, Tenements, Goods and Chattels to this Commonwealth, or such part thereof as shall be adjudged by the Justices, before whom such offense shall be tried, to be applied

A group of Massachusetts malcontents as drawn by S. Hill, 1790.

toward the support of the government of the Commonwealth; and shall be whipt Thirty-nine stripes, on the naked back, at the public whipping-post, and further imprisonment for a term not exceeding Twelve months; or once every three months during the said imprisonment, receive the same number of stripes on the naked back, at the public whipping-post as aforesaid.

Glazier Wheeler had got twenty stripes, Priscilla Wharfield twenty; the farmers were going to feel the fuller harshness of Massachusetts law. Underneath the aforesaids it meant that they had lost one item of their Bill of Rights, freedom of peaceable assembly. Now if twelve citizens armed with clubs or walking sticks did not disperse when told so, they could be killed and no one held to blame. Or if thirty persons assembled, even if carrying nothing, and did not go away, they could be killed and none held to blame.

Nor was this all. In the issue of the first week of December, the *Worcester Magazine* printed another act. It began, "Whereas the violent and outrageous opposition, which hath lately been made by armed bodies of men, in several of the counties of this commonwealth, to the constitutional authority thereof, renders it expedient and necessary," the state was going to suspend habeas corpus, as also provided for by the Massachusetts Bill of Rights. Now, as requested by Bowdoin or General Court, anyone could be imprisoned on mere suspicion, without a trial. A sheriff or deputy-sheriff or any other person authorized, could

cause to be apprehended, and committed in any jail, or

any other safe place, within the commonwealth, any person or persons whatsoever, whom the Governour and Council shall deem the safety of the commonwealth requires should be restrained of their personal liberty, or whose enlargement is dangerous thereto; any law, usage or custom to the contrary notwithstanding.

How were these dangerous persons to be apprehended? Sheriffs "shall have full power forcibly to enter any dwelling house, or any other building, in which they shall have reason to suspect any person. . . ." The government was, in short, declaring that political dissidents were criminals, and was about to begin taking political prisoners.

Quietly, once the first civil right went by the wayside, another followed it. In the first week of November, the *Worcester Magazine* reported,

Thursday last, one Elisha Capron was detected in dispersing in this town, printed hand-bills of a seditious nature, tending to promote the spirit of disaffection to the government. He was had before a magistrate, and, unable to procure the bail, was committed to prison.

Small patience as Thomas had with such goings-on, late in November in fairness he printed a petition from Daniel Shays and a "BODY OF MEN." It was a vehement protest of the imprisonment of the well-liked Job Shattuck, one of the farmers' compatriots, at Boston jail:

Your Petitioners beg leave to mention their horrour of the suspension of the privilege of the writ of Habeas Corpus, that your Excellency and your Honours may be

convinced your Petitioners are not of the wicked, dissolute and abandoned, as it is not confined to a factious few, but extended to towns and counties, and almost every individual who derives his labor from his hands or the income of a farm. That the said suspension of said privilege your Petitioners view as dangerous, if not absolutely destructive to a Republican Government. That under the cover of said privilege, your Petitioners have been informed that the eyes and breasts of women and children have been wounded, if not destroyed; the houses of the innocent broken open, their limbs mangled, their friends conveyed to gaol in another county, and now languishing (if alive) under their wounds.

Thomas placed on the facing page of the same issue of his magazine the following "Extract from a Gentleman in Buffalo, dated December 9th, 1786," which contradicted Shays's petition.

What the insurgents report about the horsemen who took Shattuck, that they put out the eye of a woman, and stabbed and cut off the breast of another, and mangled an infant in the cradle, is notoriously false, and this falsehood must be calculated to inflame the minds of people against men of the best character. No insult or injury was even intended or offered to his family; it is true they broke to pieces a gun loaded with slugs, which they found in the house . . . but no other article was meddled with.

Whom to believe? It was hard to know. Thomas himself confessed to his readers, "No dependence can be placed on many of the reports in circulation . . . thousands of falsehoods are circulated."

The bloodletting impelled the insurgents to call for a massive demonstration of solidarity in Worcester, where the Court of Common Pleas was due to sit December 5. Governor Bowdoin, determined that it was not to be interrupted, ordered the militia called out and sent an "animated and elegant address" to be read to them. This was done, and according to the *Worcester Magazine*, the reading was "answered by three huzzahs from the whole."

The huzzahs were all that the governor got for his efforts. Outnumbered by the farmers, the militia melted away, and court did not sit. But what was to have been a triumphant show of strength turned into pathetic confusion for Shays and his followers. The weather turned against them, made it impossible for reinforcements to come in from the west, and at least one man who attempted the trip froze to death on the way.

Thomas reprinted the weather report from a Boston paper, with a comment of his own:

On Monday evening last came on, and continued without intermission until Tuesday evening, as severe a snow-storm as has been experienced here for several years past. The wind, to the east, and north-east, blew exceeding heavy, and drove in the tide with such violence on Tuesday, as overflowed the pier several inches, which entering the stores on the lower part thereof, did much damage to the sugars, salt, &c. therein. . . .

During the above storm, a brig was drove ashore at Point-Shirley, and five of the hands perished. Particulars we have not learned.

Though we have mentioned it before it may again be worth observation, that storms, and thick clouds, have darkened every day, on which the enemies of our happy constitution have attempted to destroy it, by stopping the courts of justice.

The farmer-insurgents, some 1,800 of them as the magazine reported, had retreated northward and were now encamped in abandoned barracks in Rutland. Sympathizers were sending food up to them by sleigh, while they planned tactics and strategy. Also, the *Worcester Magazine* reported, "Shays posted strong guards on the heights of land; the approach of a regular army to these heights is very difficult, particularly at this season of the year."

In the meantime Boston itself lived in terror. There it was believed that only Providence in the form of the December blizzard had prevented the rebels from marching on the capital. A volunteer army of 1,500 to supplement the militia was raised to subdue the insurgents, and Boston merchants contributed nearly £6,000 to its support. Under General Benjamin Lincoln, this force now took the road to Springfield.

The news impelled the rebels to their most audacious feat. They would get to Springfield first, seize the arsenal, and with its arms defend themselves against the invasion from Boston. A local resident met some of them on the road on January 25, 1787, and sent this sworn statement to the *Worcester Magazine:*

I, JOSHUA WOODBRIDGE, of Northfield, in the county of Hampshire, and commonwealth of Massachusetts, of law ful age, testify and declare, that on the twenty-fifth day of January last, at Springfield, in said county, I met Capt. Shays on the road, marching a body of men towards Ordnance-Hill, in Springfield, where General Shepard had his troops posted;—and after a little conversation, Shays asked me, whether we had barrack room enough? I told him we had—he then said he meant, or intended to lodge in them that night: I informed him he would purchase them very hard (or dear)—he said he had a fine body of troops; I assented—but told him if he attempted to get the barracks, he would either lodge in heaven or hell—and wished him in heaven, and left him.

As of this date Lincoln's army had got only as far as Worcester. Now or never was the time to take the arsenal. It was guarded; General Shepard stood before it with a strong force of militia. But these were men of notoriously divided loyalties. A Northampton man had once written of such a confrontation: "They are our equals, our acquaintance, our brethren. . . . Impossible for us to defend ourselves against our brethren because we cannot fight them."

So the insurgents did not fear the militia. When at 250 yards Shepard ordered them to halt, they kept coming. The general knew better than to command the militia to charge. What he counted on was the disciplined crew to whom he had entrusted the artillery. When he ordered them to fire, he was obeyed.

Almost gaily Shays's men continued their forward march. It was as they expected; the shells whistled harmlessly above their heads. But a moment later all was confusion. Shepard had ordered the gunsights lowered, and the shells raked the front ranks. Three men fell dead and others wounded. The insurgents' rifles—which never fired a shot—their cutlasses, their clubs, were no defense against such a fusillade. They fled in disorder, crying murder. In his report to the governor, Shepard almost agreed with that cry:

Sir, the unhappy time has come when we have been obliged to shed blood. . . . Had I been disposed to destroy them, I might have charged upon their rear and flanks with my infantry and two field pieces and could have killed the greater part of the whole army within 25 minutes.

The *Worcester Magazine* got hold of another dispatch from the field at Springfield, this one written in the hand of Daniel Shays:

To Gen. Shepard or the Commanding Officer in Springfield Sir I Desire you to Send My Dead and Wounded men by My Flagg So that I can Burye My Dead Men and Take Care of my Wounded if not my Wounded the Dead & the Names of the Wounded by Lt. Williams Who is the Bearer of this Flagg

I am yours
Daniel Shays *Capt.*

Shays did not surrender, but this was in effect the end. By forced marches Lincoln's volunteers caught up. They were untroubled with a conflict of loyalties, fresh, and full of a heady sense of adventure. They camped at Amherst, now the site of Amherst College, and at Hadley,

View of John Hancock's luxurious estate, Boston, 1789.

where Mount Holyoke is. The *Worcester Magazine* reported that everywhere along the way "great numbers left Shays, came in and subscribed the oath of allegiance." Hundreds were taken prisoner, though except for the ringleaders they were freed when they took the oath. General Lincoln caught up with a last band of men camping at Petersham where "the whole body of insurgents scattered in all directions and fled with the greatest precipitation and disorder, leaving their pots and kettles over the fire."

Isaiah Thomas would have relished reporting the hanging of the captive insurgents. Several had been condemned, but before the sentences could be executed, John Hancock had replaced Bowdoin as governor. Though a wealthy Bostonian, Hancock sympathized with the grievances that had driven honest farmers to rebellion, and felt that the government had blundered in dealing with them. The condemned were all marched to the gallows, but a reprieve awaited them there. At long last even Shays was pardoned.

VENERATE THE PLOUGH

★ 5 ★

LET US HAVE GOVERNMENT

The dismay, the outright panic Shays's Rebellion caused had by no means been confined to Massachusetts. Among other things it had confirmed the fears of George Washington, which he now expressed in urgent correspondence to his friends:

> *For God's sakes, what is the cause of these commotions? Do they proceed from licentiousness, British influence . . . or real grievances which admit of redress? If the latter, why were they delayed until the public mind had become so agitated?*
>
> *The consequences of a lax or inefficient government are too obvious to be dwelt upon. Thirteen sovereignties pulling against each other, and all tugging at the federal head, will soon bring ruin upon the whole. . . . Let us have [government] by which our lives, liberty, and property will be secured, or let us know the worst at once.*

Washington wrote from Mount Vernon where he had hoped to spend the rest of his life. Surely he had done all that his country could expect of him during the Revolution. But winning a war was not enough; he must give himself to the even more perplexing task of winning the peace.

In late May 1787, while Massachusetts still coped with the aftermath of a rebellion, a company of dignitaries such as Philadelphia had not seen for years descended on the charming Quaker city. Aging, ailing Benjamin Franklin was carried to the statehouse in his sedan chair. Franklin's chair, the only conveyance he could endure since gout and kidney stone had become so tormenting, was a familiar sight for he lived in Philadelphia. What thrilled the people was the coach-and-four containing Washington. If he had been persuaded to leave Mount Vernon, something tremendous was about to take place.

Other notables followed, posting down the roads from New York and New England. Packets brought them in from the Carolinas to the wharfs on Water Street, for though Philadelphia was far from the sea, it was, thanks to the Delaware River, a busy port. Every state but Rhode Island was represented.

What was going on? Initially, it was an attempt to find a means of regulating the troublesome wars between the states, the duties they levied on each other, and their discrepant currencies. Even more, the delegates wanted to look into the critical situation of the "united states," and to revise the Articles of Confederation. Ultimately, however, the convention came up with a new form of national, not confederated, government, and embodied it in a constitution.

Among the first things a quorum of states' delegates, filling what was really a small room in the statehouse, adopted was a rule that "nothing spoken in this House be printed or otherwise published or communicated without leave." So it was all to be done in secrecy, and the document that the convention finally evolved was not an open covenant openly arrived at. Thomas Jefferson, then in Paris, took offense. He was sorry, he wrote, that "they began their deliberations by so abominable a precedent as that of tying up the tongues of their members. Nothing can justify this example but the innocence of their intentions, and their ignorance of the value of public discussion."

One delegate, William Paterson, had a satirical comment on the secrecy. When business called him back to New Jersey, he wrote to a colleague still on the spot. "Noisy as the wind, it is said that you are afraid of the very windows and have a man posted under them to prevent the secrets and doings from flying out."

It was true that sentries were posted at the doors and the windows kept closed. It was true that when a secret document was found lying in the hall outside the chamber, Washington, who presided, denounced such irresponsibility in a voice of thunder that made every delegate quake. It was not true that security guards were posted on Franklin when he left the hall to see that he let out no secrets. Just once he started an anecdote on the subject to a friend who was not a delegate, but caught himself in time.

Philadelphia had ten newspapers, counting two that were printed in German, but none could send a reporter to the convention. That, of course, did not silence them. The *Pennsylvania Packet* printed allegories about the prodigal son, a reference to the absent Rhode Island. It rumored a plan to divide the states up into three republics, and reported that the delegates were electing a king. This last yarn, widely circulated, drew a rare response from the convention: "While we cannot affirmatively tell you what we are doing, we can negatively tell you what we are not doing; we never once thought of a king."

With doors guarded, windows closed, the delegates sat through a long hot summer. It was a wonder that they survived it. Philadelphia was a delightful city, admired by most visitors, but it was no summer resort. Even Charleston, South Carolina, which got sea breezes and had houses built for airiness, was more comfortable.

One visitor to the city at this time was a Frenchman, Brissot de Warville, who fancied he saw in Philadelphia a city of the future. Perhaps Brissot had expected to find man in a state of nature in the New World, but in any case what he said of Philadelphia was: "When towns acquire this degree of population you must have hospitals, prisons, soldiers, police, spies, and all the sweeping train of luxury."

The first thing Brissot remarked on, as did most visitors, was Philadelphia's rectangular plan.

Philadelphia is built on a rectangular plan of long broad streets which cross each other at right angles, and run from north to south and east to west. This truly ornamental regularity is at first confusing to the stranger, for it is difficult to find one's way, especially since there are no street signs and no numbers on the doors. . . .

Besides these doors, he noted, there was often a pair of benches "where the family sits in the evening to enjoy the fresh air and watch the passersby." Brissot did not think this a good idea, "for the evening air is not always very healthy and its ill effects are not counteracted by exercise. People never take walks here; instead they have parties in the country."

Philadelphia seemed already to have problems with garbage.

Foreigners are shocked to see pigs wandering in the streets and rooting in the garbage. There is a law prohibiting them, but it is not observed. I have read in an American review [magazine] that it is both sanitary and economical to let pigs roam in the streets.

Describing Philadelphia's Quakers, he said:

The matrons wear very dark, even dismal colors, and small black bonnets with their hair simply brushed up. . . . The young women often curl their hair with so much care that they spend as much time, I am told, as they might on the most elegant toilettes. I noticed with sorrow that they wear small hats covered with silk or satin. These young Quakeresses, who are so well endowed with natural beauty . . . make themselves conspicuous by their choice of the finest linens, muslins, and silks. Their fingers play with elegant fans, and the luxury of the Orient would not disdain their fine linen. Is all this in accordance with Penn's precepts?

He was happy to meet men who lived by the old simplicity:

I have seen James Pemberton, one of the wealthiest Quakers, and a man whose virtues place him among the most respected of their leaders. His coat was threadbare but spotless; he prefers to clothe the poor and spend his money in defense of the Negroes rather than have a huge wardrobe.

You are familiar with Quaker dress: a round hat, almost always white; a coat of fairly good cloth; cotton or woolen stockings; their hair cut round and without powder. . . . On the 15th of September Quakers put on woolen stockings. This is part of their system of discipline. . . .

He had a chance too, to see a strange new machine:

I went to see an experiment near the Delaware, on a boat, the object of which is to ascend rivers against the current. The inventor was Mr. [John] Fitch, who found a company to support the expence . . . the machine which I saw appears well executed and well adapted to the design. The steam engines gives motion to three large oars of considerable force, which were to give sixty strokes per minute.

Brissot then turned his steps toward Philadelphia's House of Correction, also called the Bettering House. Here were received, he wrote, "the poor, the sick, orphans, women in travail, and persons attacked with venereal diseases. They likewise confine here vagabonds, disorderly persons, and girls of scandalous lives." The presence of foreign armies in the states, Brissot decided, had naturalized venereal disease quite quickly. Yet the House of Correction was run by Quakers and was a healthy place.

Every sick, and every poor person, has his bed well furnished. . . . Every room is lighted by windows placed opposite which introduce plenty of light. . . . These windows admit a free circulation of air: most of them open

over the fields; and as they are not very high, and are with-
out grates, it would be very easy for the prisoners to make
their escape; but the idea never enters their heads. . . .

The kitchen at the House of Correction was well kept, and did not "exhale that fetid odour which you perceive from the best kitchens in France." Though Brissot did not mention it, this kitchen was probably underground, like many he saw in Philadelphia. Perhaps it also boasted a Franklin stove. Brissot had seen one of these elsewhere, and described it as "a sort of iron affair, half stove, half fireplace . . . a detached, movable fireplace. The comfortable sight of the open fire is thus enjoyed, and the good ventilation is healthful."

Another unusual institution was the Dispensary, "which distributes medicine *gratis* to the sick who are not in a situation to purchase them."

There was also a house for the insane, although Brissot was convinced none of its inmates were "mad," to use the old-fashioned word, but rather persons "afflicted by religious melancholy or disappointed love." Their quarters were clean, but why, Brissot asked, "do they place these cells beneath the ground floor, exposed to the unwholesome humidity of the earth?" He answered his own question: "This hospital was founded at a time when little attention was thought necessary for the accommodation of fools."

If Brissot found Quaker influence still prominent in the city's institutions, Schoepf had thought German customs had a nearly equal influence. Turning to him for a moment, he had also mentioned Jews living in Philadelphia, accepted as citizens because they believed in God.

He had spoken, too, of Lutheran burial customs in the nearby country. Here the dead were buried

quietly . . . behind the house they lived in, for many landowners in America have a family burying ground in their gardens. The priesthood gains nothing by the dead unless their services are desired at burials. You may . . . be born for nothing and you may die gratis if you like; only while you live must taxes be paid.

Schoepf had been charmed by the market; he seems, too, to have been perspicacious in observing its economic structure, for he wrote,

On the evenings before the chief market days (Wednesdays and Saturdays) all the bells in the city are rung. People come from a distance, especially the Germans . . . in great covered wagons loaded down with all manner of provender, bringing with them rations for themselves and feed for their horses, for they sleep in their wagons. Numerous carts and horses bring from all directions the rich surplus of the country.

Brissot, on returning to this market, compared it with the most luxurious in the European capitals, and yet his closing description suggests it was not yet so sophisticated.

To maintain order in such a market in France would require four judges and a dozen soldiers. Here the law has no need of muskets; education and morals have done everything. Two clerks of the police walk in the market. If they suspect a pound of butter for being light, they weigh it; if light, it is seized for the use of the hospitals.

Besides, Philadelphia closed early.

By ten o'clock in the evening all is tranquil in the streets; the profound silence which reigns there is only interrupted by the voice of the watchmen, who are in small numbers, and who form the only patrol. The streets are lit by lamps, like those of London.

′ What went on in Independence Hall probably resembled a Quaker meeting to outsiders hungry for news. For all one knew the members sat in unbroken silence waiting for the spirit to move. Even history is ignorant of many details, dependent upon reminiscence uttered many years later from sometimes questionable memory, and from the notes taken by a few delegates, notably James Madison.

Secrecy was probably a wise rule, Thomas Jefferson to the contrary. The spirit did move within the hall; it moved mightily, often with heat and passion. Had the papers at once published what was said, delegates might have been condemned to that consistency which Emerson called "the hobgoblin of little minds," forced to defend random and sometimes rash remarks that were only a stage in the evolution of their thinking.

Of all the problems that faced the convention, none was more complex, more troublesome, than that presented by the existence of slavery. The delegates did not solve it. Their failure to do so would in little more than half a century blow their hard-won union apart. In the meantime the long debate raised explosive passions.

The subject came up in three connections: (1) How was representation to be proportioned in the lower house of Congress? (2) Was the slave trade from Africa to be stopped or continued? and (3) On what imported articles

A 1790 caricature. Financier Robert Morris, moneybag in hand, drags Congress to Philadelphia.

should federal taxes be levied? The word slave never found its way into the Constitution, but the convention dialogue on the subject was quite bald.

Question 1 had first raised difficulties quite aside from the complication of slavery. The smaller states cherished the veto power the Articles of Confederation had given them by allowing each state one vote. The Delaware delegates had instructions to withdraw if any other arrangement was considered. Being men of sound common sense they did not. They assumed, correctly as it turned out, that their small state would be pacified by the compromise adopted: equal representation in the Senate, "proportional" representation in the House.

But this compromise raised another problem in connection with slavery that seemed insoluble. Proportional representation on what basis? James Wilson of Pennsylvania introduced a method:

. . . add, after the words "equitable ratio of representation" the words following, "in proportion to the whole number of white and other free citizens and inhabitants of every age, sex and condition, including those bound to servitude for a term of years, and three fifths of all other persons not comprehended in the foregoing description, except Indians not paying taxes.

In other words, a black person, not comprehended in the foregoing description since not even mentioned, was to be considered not a whole person, but three fifths of a person. Elbridge Gerry (Massachusetts) objected: "Mr. Gerry thought property not the rule of representation.

Why then should blacks, who were property in the South, be in the rule of representation more than the cattle and horses of the north?"

But perhaps representation *should* be based on property? William Paterson (New Jersey) vetoed that idea. He

considered the proposed estimate [three-fifths] for the future according to the combined rule of numbers and wealth as too vague. . . . He could regard Negro slaves in no light but as property. They are not free agents, have no personal liberty, no faculty of acquiring property, but on the contrary are themselves property, and like other property, entirely at the will of the master. Has a man in Virginia a number of votes in proportion to the number of his slaves? And if Negroes are not represented in the states to which they belong, why should they be represented in the general government?

What is the true principle of representation? It is an expedient by which an assembly of certain individuals chosen by the people is substituted in place of the inconvenient meeting of the people themselves. If such a meeting of the people was actually to take place, would the slaves vote? They would not. Why then should they be represented?

The two South Carolina delegates, Pierce Butler and General Charles C. Pinckney, had quite different objects; they

insisted that blacks be included in the rules of representation equally with the Whites, and for that purpose moved that the words "three-fifths" be struck out. . . .

Mr. Butler insisted that the labor of a slave in South Carolina was as productive and valuable as that of a freeman in Massachusetts, that as wealth was the great means of defense and utility to the nation, they were equally valuable to it with freemen; and that consequently an equal representation ought to be allowed for them in a government which was instituted principally for the protection of property. . . .

Virginian George Mason, an active worker for abolition, opposed the South Carolinians' motion.

Mr. Mason could not agree to the motion, notwithstanding it was favorable to Virginia because he thought it unjust. It was certain that the slaves were valuable, as they raised the value of the land, increased the exports and imports, and of course the revenue; would supply the means of feeding and supporting an army, and might in cases of emergency become themselves soldiers.

As in these important respects they were useful to the community at large, they ought not to be excluded from the estimate of representation. He could not, however, regard them [in their enslaved condition] as equal to freemen and could not vote for them as such. He added as worthy of remark, that the Southern states have this peculiar species of property, over and above the other species of property common to all the states.

Only South Carolina, Delaware, and Georgia voted for equality of representation. Debate continued on the proposition that blacks—Isaac Smith, for example—be counted as three fifths of a man. At the idea, Pennsylvania's Gouverneur Morris

was compelled to declare himself reduced to the dilemma of doing injustice to the Southern states or to human nature, and he must therefore do it to the former. For he would never agree to give such encouragement to the slave trade as would be given by allowing them a representation for their Negroes, and he did not believe those states would ever confederate on terms that would deprive them of that trade.

Through the dog days of July the debate went on in the breathless hall. At one point the aged Benjamin Franklin urged that the assembly try invoking God. "God governs in the affairs of men. And if a sparrow cannot fall to the ground without His notice, is it probable that an empire can rise without His aid?"

Washington was presiding (and it is worth noting that he was called "President" even before he became one); he joined no debate and his voice was seldom heard. But inwardly he was close to despair, especially when, on July 12, William Richardson Davie (North Carolina) threatened to withdraw his delegation.

Mr. Davie . . . saw that it was meant by some gentlemen to deprive the Southern states of any shape of representation for their blacks. He was sure that North Carolina would never confederate on any terms that did not rate them at least as three fifths. If the Eastern states meant to exclude them altogether the business was at an end.

Gouverneur Morris again faced the moral dilemma:

He came here to form a compact for the good of America. He was ready to do so with all the states; he hoped and believed that all would enter into such a compact. If they would not, he was ready to join with any state that would. But as the compact was to be voluntary, it is in vain for the Eastern states to insist on what the Southern states will never agree to. It is equally vain for the latter to require what the other states can never admit; and he verily believed that the people of Pennsylvania will never agree to a representation of Negroes.

Apparently he forgot that, in his state, free Negroes had the vote.

On July 13 the issue was settled. The notion of representation based on property was discarded; it would be based on population, as determined by periodic census, and "the persons of other descriptions" would be reckoned on a three-fifths basis.

But the debate on slavery was only beginning. Now rose question 2, the African slave trade. The Revolution had ended it, and only one state, Georgia, the only colony founded with the provision that slavery be forever excluded, had resumed it. "Forever" had lasted not quite twenty years. Now South Carolina, whose rice and indigo plantations took a heavy toll of human life, also planned to resume importation.

Rufus King (Massachusetts) took the stand:

The admission of slaves [as imports] was a most grating circumstance to his mind, and he believed would be so to a great part of the people of America. He had not made a strenuous opposition to it heretofore because he had hoped that this concession [on representation] would have produced a readiness . . . to strengthen the general government and to mark a full confidence in it. The report under consideration had . . . put an end to all these hopes.

In two great points the hands of the legislature were absolutely tied. [Suppose] the importation of slaves could not be prohibited—[and suppose] exports could not be taxed. Is this reasonable? What are the great objects of the general system? 1. Defense against foreign invasion. 2. Against internal sedition. Shall all the states then be bound to defend each; and shall each be at liberty to introduce a weakness which will render defense more difficult? Shall one part of the U.S. be bound to defend another part, and that other part be at liberty not only to increase its own danger, but to withhold the compensation for the burden?

If slaves are to be imported, shall not the exports produced by their labor supply a revenue the better to enable the general government to defend their masters? There was so much inequality and unreasonableness in all this that the people of the northern states could never be reconciled. . . .

Morris spoke again, beginning his argument with the nefarious effects of the slave traffic.

He would never concur in upholding domestic slavery. It was a nefarious institution—it was the curse of heaven on the states where it prevailed. Compare the free regions of the Middle States, where a rich and noble cultivation marks the prosperity and happiness of the people, with the misery and poverty which overspread the barren wastes of Virginia, Maryland, and the other states having slaves. Travel through ye whole continent and you behold the prospect continually varying with the appearance and disappearance of slavery. The moment ye leave ye Eastern states and enter New York, the effects of the institution become visible; passing through the Jerseys and entering Pennsylvania, every criterion of superior improvement witnesses the change. Proceed southwardly, and every step ye take through ye great regions of slaves presents a desert increasing with ye increasing proportion of these wretched beings. . . .

The houses in this city, Philadelphia, are worth more than all the wretched slaves which cover the rice swamps of South Carolina. The admission of slaves into the representation when fairly explained comes to this: that the inhabitant of Georgia and South Carolina who goes to the coast of Africa, and in defiance of the most sacred laws of humanity tears away his fellow creatures from their dearest connections and damns them to the most cruel bondage, shall have more votes in a government instituted for the protection of the rights of mankind than the citizen of Pennsylvania or New Jersey, who view with a laudable horror so nefarious a practice.

Like Rufus King, Morris next alluded to another troublesome point being hammered out in this convention, the proposition that the militia would no longer be under state but under federal control. At long range he foresaw Harper's Ferry, where a slave rebellion was put down by federal troops. (Oddly enough, though, the first use to which the federal government was going to put the combined militias of several states was against a part of his own Pennsylvania.)

And what is the proposed compensation of the northern states for a sacrifice of every principle of right, of every impulse of humanity? They are to bind themselves to march their militia for the defense of the southern states; for their defense against those very slaves. . . .

Morris's contemptuous reference to the slave-holding states did not rankle Virginia's Mason. He cited England's refusal up to the Revolution to let Virginia end the slave trade, a trade he called an "infernal" traffic.

Maryland and Virginia [he said] had already prohibited the importation of slaves expressly. North Carolina had done the same in substance. All this would be in vain if South Carolina and Georgia be at liberty to import. The western people are already calling out for slaves for their new lands, and will fill that country with slaves if they can be got through South Carolina and Georgia.

In addition, Mason lamented "some of our Eastern brethren had from a lust of gain embarked in this nefarious traffic." One of the "Eastern brethren," Oliver Ellsworth (Connecticut), spoke up:

As he had never owned a slave [he] could not judge of the effects of slavery on character. He said, however, that if it was to be considered in a moral light, we ought to go further and free those already in the country.

As slaves also multiply so fast in Virginia and Maryland that it is cheaper to raise than import them, whilst in the sickly rice swamps foreign supplies are necessary, if we go no farther than is urged we shall be unjust towards South Carolina and Georgia. Let us not intermeddle. As population increases, poor laborers will be so plenty as to render slaves useless. Slavery in time will not be a speck in our country.

He was an optimist. Slavery would remain much more than "a speck in our country." But his "let us not intermeddle" carried the day, especially when ominous threats came from the Carolinas.

Said General Pinckney:

South Carolina and Georgia cannot do without slaves. As to Virginia, she will gain by stopping the importations. Her slaves will rise in value and she has more than she wants. . . . He admitted it to be reasonable that the slaves should be dutied like other imports, but should consider a rejection of the clause as an exclusion of South Carolina from the Union.

His colleague, John Rutledge, added:

If the convention thinks that North Carolina, South Carolina, and Georgia will ever agree to the plan unless their right to import slaves be untouched, the expectation is vain. The people of those states will never be such fools as to give up so important an interest.

Gouverneur Morris recommended a "bargain among the northern and southern states," and so it was done, another great compromise in the Constitution. The importation of slaves would not be cut off before January 1808; in the meantime (question 3) the importers would pay a duty of up to ten dollars on each slave.

Penmanship guide used in New England school in the 1790s. One of the captions reads "By virtuous actions we our lives maintain which after death our monuments remain." The last caption says "Vive La Plume" —the pen is mightier than the sword.

By September the Constitution was ready for signing. Compromise had been hammered out, and an impressive federal government had been designed, divided into three departments: executive, legislative, and judicial. It had a preamble beginning not with the old phrase "the states of," but with the significant words "We the People." It would operate directly upon human beings instead of upon states.

Not every delegate signed. There had always been a strong minority of dissent with many of the Constitution's provisions, even with its whole philosophy. Among those who refused to sign were George Mason and Elbridge Gerry. Soon, as the states began to hold ratifying conventions, they would side with the Anti-Federalists, those who opposed, and vehemently, the proposed Constitution. Some who signed dissented still; but the Constitution existed as yet only on paper. It would have no validity until it had been ratified by a majority of the states, and this process would not be carried out in secrecy.

Many delegates had already signed the Declaration of Independence or the Articles of Confederation. A farmer and a shoemaker from Connecticut, Roger Sherman, was the only man who could claim signing all three documents.

Benjamin Franklin had as many doubts as any man, but he signed and made a rare remark, which Madison recorded:

Whilst the last members were signing it, Doctor Franklin, looking towards the President's Chair at the back of which a rising sun happened to be painted, observed to a few members near him that painters had found it difficult to distinguish in their art a rising from a setting sun. I have, said he, often and often in the course of the session and the vicissitudes of my hopes and fears as to its issue, looked at that behind the President without being able to tell whether it was rising or setting; but now at length I have the happiness to know that it is a rising and not a setting sun.

★ | 6 | ★

FOUR WEEKS IN BOSTON

The next eight months saw feverish political activity. For the Constitution to go into effect, nine of the thirteen states had to ratify it, not through their legislatures, but by the people themselves as represented by their elected delegates, who would attend conventions assembled for the purpose.

Nevertheless, the state legislatures had to act first. They had to authorize state conventions and arrange for local elections of delegates. The Pennsylvania assembly at first showed reluctance to do so; Rhode Island refused outright. Instead of calling a convention Rhode Island referred the question of ratification to its town meetings, and these turned it down by a vote of nearly ten to one. Was that going to be the verdict of "We the People"?

Elsewhere, election of delegates was preceded by impassioned debate. In New England, many delegates were sent to the conventions with specific instructions on how they were to vote when they got there. One Massachusetts delegate, who defended the Constitution in debate on the floor, nevertheless voted against it: to him his instructions were more binding than his convictions. New Hampshire delegates were so bewildered by the wide range of opinion they encountered when they met that they adjourned the convention to give themselves time to go home and consult their constituents.

There was less difficulty in other states. Delaware, New Jersey, and Georgia conventions rubber-stamped the Constitution by unanimous vote. In other states the debates were prolonged and gave rise to party politics. Nowhere did the Constitution provide for political parties, but they were to become as important to the future as the document itself. Already they had names: those favoring ratification called themselves *Federalists*; the opposition took the name of *Anti-Federalists*.

In Pennsylvania, where the convention opened debate in November 1787, one Philadelphian denounced what looked like a rush to ratify in a letter to George Mason. The Philadelphian wrote,

I cannot imagine why the people in this city are so verry anxious to have it adopted instantly before it can be digested and deliberately considered. If you were only here to see and hear these people, to observe the Means they are using to effect this purpose, to hear the tories declaring they will draw the Sword in its defence, to see the Quakers running about signing declarations and Petitions in favor of it before the[y] have time to examine it, to see gentlemen running into the Country and neighboring towns haranguing the rabble. I say were you to see and hear these things as I do you would say with me that the verry Soul of confidence ought to change into distrust.

In the Virginia convention, several months later, delegate William Grayson wittily protested the exaggerations of the Federalists, who forecast destruction for the country if the Constitution were not ratified at once and without amendments. Grayson argued:

We are now told by the honorable gentlemen that we shall have wars and rumors of wars, that every calamity is to attend us, and that we shall be ruined and disunited forever unless we adopt their Constitution. Pennsylvania and Maryland are to fall upon us from the north, like the Goths and Vandals of old; the Algerines, whose flat-sided vessels never came farther than Madeira, are to fill the Chesapeak with mighty fleets and to attack us on our front; the Indians are to invade us with numerous armies on our rear, in order to convert our cleared lands into hunting-grounds; and the Carolinians from the south (mounted on alligators I presume) are to come and destroy our cornfields and eat up our little children. These, sir, are the mighty dangers which await us if we reject.

How did they conduct a political campaign without the aid of trained campaign managers, television, and radio? There were substitutes adequate to the time. The New England town meeting was at least the equivalent of the modern talk show, and the press was open to a variety of opinion. Federalists contributed pieces signed by classic names like Publius and Caesar; their opponents addressed the public over signatures like Agrippa, Candidus, and Centinel.

The most distinguished and widely circulated of the newspaper articles written during the eight months the conventions were in session were those by Publius in the *New York Journal*. Publius was sometimes James Madison and sometimes John Jay, but mostly he was Alexander

The thirteen states drawing the chariot of Union; from Bickerstaff's Boston Almanack, 1788.

Hamilton, a "campaign manager" whose techniques Madison Avenue might envy. Their essays, now known as *The Federalist Papers*, though written in haste, were so brilliantly reasoned that they have ever since been recognized as a major work of American political science, ranking next to the Constitution itself and the Declaration of Independence. To this day they are studied and cited by lawyers and even by members of the Supreme Court in analyzing the powers of President and Congress.

However brilliant, Publius did not immediately sway the general public to his point of view. The widespread publication of his articles antagonized many who felt that the Federalists were being permitted to monopolize the press. They were partly right; few papers were printed outside the cities, and such city dwellers as merchants, bankers, import-exporters, and small businessmen were in favor of the strong central government promised by the Constitution. Those who opposed it felt that their views were inadequately represented, and charged political intimidation of the editors, sometimes with reason. The *Philadelphia Herald,* the *Boston Morning Herald,* and New York City's *Morning Post* had all experienced boycotts by Federalist subscribers and advertisers when they printed denunciations of the Constitution. A South Carolina Anti-Federalist complained that in Charleston,

The printers are, in general, British journeymen, or poor citizens, who are afraid to offend the great men, or Merchants who could work their ruin. Thus with us the press is in the hands of a junto, and the Printers, with most servile insolence discouraged opposition and pushed forward publications in its favor, for no one wrote against it.

In South Carolina it was claimed that four-fifths of that state opposed the Constitution. Why then did South Carolina ratify? One delegate to the convention in Charleston claimed that the "despotic laws" could be rammed "down their throats [only] with the point of bayonets." Yet of the seven delegates from his own parish four voted aye. Had the country folk been railroaded? Were they cowed by the superior education and wealth of the coastal Federalists? Or was it simply lack of organization? Perhaps a little of each.

The Charleston delegate explained:

We in the opposition had not, previous to our meeting, either wrote, or spoke hardly a word against it, nor took any one step in the matter. We had no principle of concert or union, while its friends and abettors left no expedient untried to push it forward. [These were] all the rich leading men along the sea coast and rice settlements with few exceptions, Lawyers, Physicians and Divines; the Merchants, mechanicks, the Populace and mob of Charleston.

Also, he hinted darkly, "The Merchants and leading men kept open house for the back and low country members during the whole time the Convention sat."

All the towns of Massachusetts, even those most active in Shays's Rebellion, were represented in the convention which met in Boston in the mild January of 1788. There were 364 delegates, too many to be comfortably seated in the old brick state house, which had been the Town House in colonial times. They moved their deliberations to the Brattle Street Church, and finally to a meeting-house with a gallery capacious enough to admit the public.

It was on Long Lane, which as a result of what the convention accomplished was renamed Federal Street. In authorizing the convention the legislature had debated the wisdom of excluding delegates who had backed Daniel Shays. In the end they excluded only one, William Whiting, a judge who had written in defense of the people's right to close the courts. The loss of this man was a blow; in him the Anti-Federalists would have had their most articulate spokesman. Even so, when they assembled on January 9, the Anti-Federalists probably commanded a clear majority, and were determined to smother the Constitution with a resounding nay.

Would the Federalists, the propertied men of the East, stop at anything to balk them? The Anti-Federalists' worst suspicions were confirmed when they read an item in the *Boston Gazette* headed "Bribery and Corruption."

The most diabolical plan is on foot to corrupt the members of the convention who oppose the adoption of the new constitution. Large sums of money have been brought in from a neighboring state for that purpose, contributed by the wealthy. If so, is it not probable that there may be collections for the same accursed purpose nearer Home?

But the editor was summoned to explain this story. A contributor to his paper confessed: it was a rumor only; he had heard of influences being brought to bear on an outspoken Maine delegate, and of "a bag of money" sent in from Rhode Island.

Bribery had been, in fact, no part of the Federalists' plans. What they needed was time—to work on the undecided delegates. To this end they arranged that the Constitution be discussed paragraph by paragraph, a technique that strung out the convention for thirty-eight interminable days. This exasperated the Anti-Federalist delegates from the western counties and the three from Maine, still a part of Massachusetts, who had been sufficiently annoyed at having to meet in Boston at all. William Widgery of Maine lost his patience. He protested the expense of living in Boston, and demanded that the convention move more rapidly. He incurred an august reproof from the old patriot Samuel Adams: "We ought not to be stingy of our time and the public's money when so important an object demands them." Adams added that, "He was sorry for the gentleman's necessities; but he would rather support the gentlemen who were so necessitated or lend them money to do it than that they should hurry so great a subject."

Did Adams' offer constitute "bribery and corruption," or the wining and dining hinted at in South Carolina? Hardly. Anyone who knew Sam Adams, and that was everybody, knew that he was at least as lean about the pocketbook as poor Widgery. He had failed in every business he undertook until he found his vocation in the struggle against King George, and that had brought him fame but not fortune.

Endorsement from such a prominent figure would have been sought after in any political campaign, and the Federalists had worried about Sam Adams, whose misgivings about the Constitution they well knew. Thus they had arranged, just before the convention, a political rally of shipwrights and mechanics at Boston's Green Dragon Tavern. These favored the Constitution and so expressed themselves in a resolution they drew up at the Green Dragon. But it was a cleverer thing by far when Paul Revere carried their resolution away and gave it to Sam Adams. The two had a conversation. Adams didn't believe the resolution was true at first, and cross-examined Paul Revere skeptically:

> "How many mechanics were at the Green Dragon when this resolution passed?"
> "More, sir, than the Green Dragon could hold."
> "And where were the rest, Mr. Revere?"
> "In the street, sir."
> "And how many were in the street?"
> "More, sir, than there are stars in the sky."

Another old patriot who was believed to have doubts about the Constitution was the new Massachusetts governor, John Hancock. He had been elected president of the convention, but gout kept him from taking the podium until it was half over. Hancock's affliction was famous; it flared up so regularly, so dependably in moments of uncertainty that it was known as his "diplomatic gout." Not until speakers like former Governor Bowdoin and Rufus King had by their able defense of the Constitution allayed his uneasiness did Hancock's gout permit him to attend.

Endorsements by the illustrious did not always work as a political tactic. Some of the Massachusetts delegates were remarkably stubborn, and not to be cowed by eminence. General Thompson from Maine denounced the Constitution's recognition of slavery, and with it, slaveowner George Washington:

Shall it be said that after we have established our own independence and freedom we make slaves of others? Oh Washington, what a name has he had! How he has immortalized himself! But he holds those in slavery who have as good a right to be free as he has. He is still for self; and in my opinion his character has sunk fifty percent.

A group of "Yeomen of Massachusetts," who wrote in to the Massachusetts *Guardian* on January 25, 1788, agreed:

Another thing they tell us, that the constitution must be good from the characters which composed the Convention that framed it. It is graced with the names of a Washington and a Franklin. Illustrious names, we know —worthy characters in civil society. Yet we cannot suppose them to be infallible guides; neither yet that a man must necessarily incur guilt to himself merely by dissenting from them in opinion.

We cannot think the noble general has the same ideas with ourselves, with regard to the rules of right and wrong. We cannot think he acts a very consistent part, or did through the whole of the contest with Great Britain. Notwithstanding he wielded the sword in defense of American liberty, yet at the same time was, and is to this day, living upon the labors of several hundreds of miserable Africans, as free born as himself; and some of them very likely descended from parents, who in point and property and dignity in their own country, might cope with any man in America. We do not conceive we are to be overborne by the weight of any names, however revered. "ALL MEN ARE BORN FREE AND EQUAL."

These Massachusetts yeomen were not going to let any holier-than-thou aristocrats lord it over them. However rustic, salty, or ungrammatical their speech, and however simple their daily concerns as they farmed, they were democrats and they wanted to live in a democracy. No Federalist would have touched the word democracy with a ten-foot pole, although in the practical business of caucusing and debating on the convention floor, the learned Federalists quickly began to appreciate the fact that their classical citations had small influence upon such yeomen. At the outset defenders of the Constitution had fortified their arguments with examples from ancient Greece and Rome, until they got tartly dressed down by a Mr. Randall who said that "the quoting of ancient history was no more to the purpose than to tell how our forefathers dug clams at Plymouth." Biblical allusions moved another delegate to remark that "he would not trust a flock of Moseses." So the Federalists learned to make their similes more homely.

But the cut about democracy went deeper than rhetoric. Many Anti-Federalists were fearful that the proposed Constitution was going to favor aristocrats and rich urbanites, and leave out the common folk—farmers, debtors, and other plain people. This fear was at the heart of much Anti-Federalist resentment against the Constitution. In Massachusetts it was clearly expressed by delegate "Daddy" Singletarry, long a representative to Massachusetts General Court from the town of Sutton. Always known for his salty utterance, Singletarry made a picturesque speech in opposition. "Mr. President," he began, addressing Governor John Hancock, standing up there now that his gout had disappeared,

I should not have troubled the convention again if some gentlemen had not called on them that were on the stage at the beginning of our troubles, in the year 1775. I was one of them . . . and I say that if anybody had proposed such a constitution as this in that day it would have been thrown away at once. . . . We contended with Great Britain, some said, for a threepenny duty on tea; but it was not that. It was because they claimed a right to tax us and bind us in all cases whatever. And does not this constitution do the same? Does it not take away all we have —all our property? Does it not lay all taxes, duties, imposts, and excises? And what more have we to give? . . .

These lawyers and men of learning and moneyed men that talk so finely, and gloss over matters so smoothly, to make us poor illiterate people swallow down the pill, expect to get into Congress themselves; they expect to be the managers of this constitution, and get all the power and all the money into their own hands, and then they will swallow up all us little folks like the great Leviathan, Mr. President; yes, just as the whale swallowed Jonah.

If what he said was true, the whale, not long after, did swallow Jonah in Massachusetts. After thirty-eight days of prolonged debate, the Federalists succeeded in turning the vote to their favor. The state voted 187 for the Constitution, 168 against it. Massachusetts had ratified.

In New York, too, where the convention was held between June 17 and July 26, the Anti-Federalists were strong. When debate opened, they had 46 delegates, the Federalists 19. Debate was fierce, and so was propagandizing and pamphleteering. Alexander Hamilton was active in New York City and the southern part of the state, and

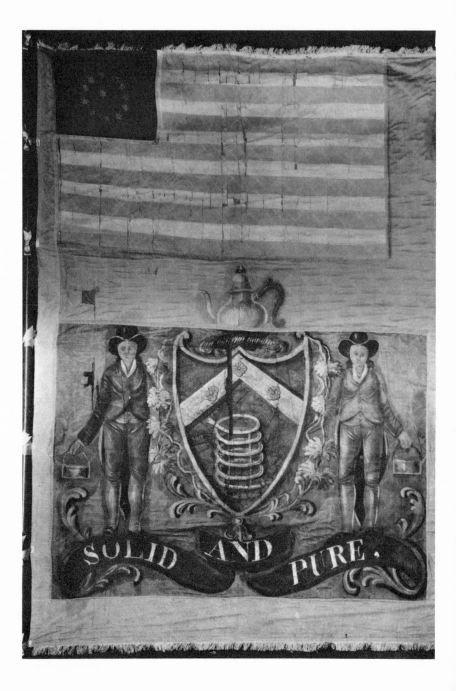

SOLID AND PURE,

Flag carried by pewterers in New York City procession celebrating ratification of the Constitution, July 23, 1788. Note leather aprons worn by craftsmen at work.

managed to win over some of the opposition. He was not above duplicity, or so one New York Anti-Federalist alleged. This New Yorker wrote, "You would be surprised if you know the Man, what an *amazing Republican* Hamilton wishes to make himself be considered." The writer added ominously, "But he is known."

A more thoughtful extension of the argument, that the Constitution would favor aristocrats and merchants and forget the rest, was delivered in debate at New York by the able Melancthon Smith. Federalist arguments at the convention so far, Smith declared, had not affected his low opinion of the Constitution in the least. Or rather, "if my Sentiments are altered it is to think it worse." Politically astute, Melancthon Smith, too, claimed that the very process of large popular elections would make it inevitable that the elite would win political power. A farseeing man, Melancthon Smith told the delegates:

The influence of the great will generally enable them to succeed in elections. It will be difficult to combine a district of country containing 30,000 or 40,000 inhabitants, frame your election laws as you please, in any other character, unless it be in one of conspicuous, military, popular, civil, or legal talents. The great easily form associations; the poor and middling classes form them with difficulty.

If the elections be by plurality . . . it is almost certain none but the great will be chosen—for they easily unite their interest; the common people will divide, and their divisions will be promoted by the others. There will scarcely be a chance for their uniting in any other but some great man, unless in some popular demagogue, who will probably be destitute of principle. A substantial yeoman of sense and discernment will hardly ever be chosen.

A merchants office as shown by a late 18th century engraving.

. . . The government will fall into the hands of the few and the great.

In spite of such strong opposition, New York finally ratified by the slim margin of three votes on July 26— the count was 30 to 27. The result was something of a marvel, engineered largely by Alexander Hamilton. In the closing days of debate, Hamilton had personally arranged for an express messenger to carry the news to New York State that New Hampshire had just ratified, the implication being that the Constitution was already in operation and a "no" vote would make no difference. But New York ratified only after the Federalists had guaranteed that there would be amendments to the Constitution.

The amendments demanded were a bill of rights. In most state conventions, not only Anti-Federalists but also some Federalists had protested that the Constitution was defective; it gave the individual no protection against oppression by the government. Many had wanted to make ratification contingent on such guarantees. But amendments could not be adopted without a constitutionally elected Congress to pass them. In the end the objections were overruled. Only North Carolina, whose convention adjourned without either ratifying or rejecting the Constitution, waited for the defect to be remedied.

The Constitution apparently offered no protection of freedom of speech, of religion, of peaceable assembly, such as had been given to the English in 1688 by their Bill of Rights. Why did it need one, asked the hard-line Federalists? The individual state constitutions, mostly drawn up after the Declaration of Independence, already had such bills. Virginia's went back to 1776. The Massachusetts constitution, drawn up the same year, was not accepted by the voters until 1780 when a very detailed bill of rights was added. Under these circumstances was not a federal bill redundant?

Many delegates in the ratifying conventions did not think so. For one thing they were uncertain where federal power ended and state authority began. They demanded an amendment clarifying this point. They wanted other rights spelled out in plain English. Until this was done, was not "Daddy" Singletarry justified in his fear that the money men would "swallow up all us little folks . . . just as the whale swallowed Jonah"? It was not that Singletarry begrudged the great men their fortunes or their classical educations, but let them not be empowered to interfere with what made his own life decent and human. Give him amendments that would secure him from unreasonable arrest, double jeopardy, or trial by torture. Give him a guarantee that he could think for himself and express his thoughts to his fellows in town meeting or in the press without fear of arrest. Give him leave to worship as he pleased, as Quaker, Anglican, Baptist, Jew— or not to worship at all. Give him these and he need not fear the great men. In a country so young and so fruitful, an ocean removed from its enemies, who knew but that one day his sons might not join the ranks of the great men?

Singletarry's views were eloquently defended by a Virginian of the very class he feared. Richard Henry Lee, of manorial Stratford, did not participate in the Virginia convention in the late spring of 1788, but his sentiments did. They had been published several months earlier in a forty-page pamphlet entitled *Letters from a Federal Farmer to the Republican.* In the debates on the convention floor between Federalist James Madison and his fiery opponent Patrick Henry, *Federal Farmer* had almost as much influence on Henry as Hamilton's Publius had on Madison.

When the Virginia convention opened, the two parties were about evenly divided. Oddly enough, though in most states the plain folks in the western sections were solidly opposed to the Constitution, here it was otherwise. The frontier mountain people in that part of the state that was to become Kentucky were solidly for the Constitution. They wanted a strong central government to protect them against the Indians and get rid of the hated English forts in the Northwest Territory. Their opponents on ratification were in the middle of the state and in Tidewater, the wealthy, slave-holding planters.

Lee himself was less against the Constitution than against its adoption without a bill of rights. His arguments began:

All wise and prudent people in forming constitutions have drawn the line and carefully described the powers parted with and the powers preserved. . . . It is true we are not disposed to differ much at present about religion; but when we are making a constitution it is to be hoped for ages and millions yet unborn, why not establish the free exercise of religion as part of the national compact?

With a sense of noblesse oblige the Virginia aristocrat advocated that which most Federalists avoided, the concept of democracy. As he saw it, the Constitution might establish a republic, but without a bill of rights it would not be a democracy. Could the proposed House of Representatives, elected on a basis of one to every 50,000 people, adequately represent its constituents?

I have no idea that the interests, feelings, and opinions of these four millions of people, especially touching internal taxation, can be collected in such a house. In the nature of things, nine times out of ten, men of the elevated classes in the community only can be chosen . . . the people of this country, in one sense, may all be democratic; but if we make the proper distinction between the few men of wealth and abilities, and consider them, as we ought, the natural aristocracy of the country, and the great body of people, the middle and lower classes, as the democracy, this federal representative branch will have but very little democracy in it.

Thus, a bill of rights would be a further kind of representation for the common people. It would also be a necessary protection

to secure the people against the fatal effects of corruption and influence. The powers of making any law will be in the [hands of a few] relative to the important objects enumerated in the Constitution. Where there is a small representation, a sufficient number to carry any measure, may, with ease, be influenced by bribes, offices and civilities; they [may] easily form private juntos, and out-door meetings, agree on measures, and carry them by silent votes.

My Fancy Flies Free

My Fancy Flies Free is an ode to freedom. It was brought to America by German immigrants in the 18th century.

I think of what I please
    And what gives me pleasure;
The world of which I dream
    Is made to my own measure.
My heart's own desire
    Is a masterless fire,
That's the way it shall be,
    My fancy flies free.

Pour out the red wine
    For my darling and me;
The green earth now is mine
    And contented I'll be;
I am not alone
    If a bottle I own
And my loved one's by me;
    My fancy flies free.

The highest stone wall
    Or well-guarded jail,
Resistless will fall
    And nothing avail.
My thought is so swift
    It makes a deep rift
In the thick masonry;
    My fancy flies free.

Farewell then to sadness
    And meaningless care;
Instead welcome gladness
    And happy you'll fare.
Your soul fill with laughter
    And sing ever after,
And know it shall be,
    Our fancy flies free!

Federal Farmer regarded the trial by jury not only as a safeguard to fair trials, but again as further representation for the common man in his hierarchical and centralized government. "The trial by jury is very important," Lee wrote:

It is essential in every free country, that common people should have a part and share of influence, in the judicial as well as in the legislative department. To hold open to them the offices of senators, judges, and offices to fill which an expensive education is required, cannot answer any valuable purpose for them; they are not in a situation to be brought forward and to fill these offices; these, and many other offices of any considerable importance will be occupied by the few. The few, the well born, &c. as Mr. [John] Adams calls them, in judicial decisions as well as in legislation, are generally disposed and very naturally too, to favour those of their own description. . . . I am very sorry that a few of our countrymen should consider jurors and representatives in a different point of view, as ignorant and troublesome bodies, which ought not to have any share in the concerns of government.

A trial face-to-face with a jury, and in the vicinity of the place where the alleged crime was committed, was also crucial at getting at the truth. Wrote Lee:

Nothing can be more essential than the cross-examining witnesses, and generally before the triers of the facts in question. The common people can establish facts with much more ease with oral than written evidence; when trials of facts are removed to a distance from the homes of the parties and witnesses, oral evidence becomes intolerably expensive, and the parties must depend on written evidence, which to the common people is expensive and almost useless; it must be frequently taken ex parte [from one side only] and but very seldom leads to the proper discovery of truth.

Several states' conventions, and many Anti-Federalists, asserted that a prohibition against standing armies should also be included in a bill of rights. *Federal Farmer* shared this conviction, and was fearful of the connection between the purse and sword in the central government.

The power in the general government to lay and collect internal taxes, will render its powers respecting armies, navies and the militia, the more exceptionable. . . . I see so many men in America fond of a standing army, and especially among those who probably will have a large share in administering the federal system; it is very evident to me, that we shall have a large standing army, as soon as the monies to support them can be possibly found.

Lee elaborated with a prediction and a warning. If prohibition of standing armies was not included in a bill of rights,

It is true, the yeomanry of the country possess the lands, the wealth of the property, possess arms, and are too strong a body of men to be openly offended and, therefore, it is urged, they will take care of themselves, that men who shall govern will not dare pay any disrespect to their opinions. [But] It is easily perceived, that if they have not their proper negative upon passing laws in congress, or on the passage of laws relative to taxes and armies they may in twenty or thirty years by means imperceptible to them, be totally deprived of that boasted wealth and strength; This may be done in a great measure by congress, if disposed to do it, by modelling [organizing] the militia. Should one-fifth or one-eighth part of the men capable of bearing arms, be made a select militia, as has been proposed, and those the young and ardent part of the community, possessed of but little or no property, and all the others put upon a plan that will render them of no importance, the former will answer all the purposes of an army, while the latter will be defenceless.

In urging his fellow Virginians not to be too hasty about accepting the proposed Constitution without revisions, *Federal Farmer* warned them against political rhetoric, which had characterized the campaigning.

When we want a man to change his condition we describe it as wretched, miserable, and despised; and draw a pleasing picture of that which we would have him assume. And when we wish the contrary, we reverse our descriptions. . . .
It is natural for men, who wish to hasten adoption of a measure, to tell us, now is the crisis—now is the critical moment which must be seized or all will be lost; and to shut the door against free enquiry, whenever conscious the thing presented has difficulties in it, which time and investigation will probably discover. This has been the custom of tyrants, and their dependents in all ages.

Despite Lee's reservations, the Virginia convention

adopted the Constitution, on June 25 by a vote of 89 to 79. And with ratification by both Virginia and New York, the Constitution went into effect. It had been passed without amendments, but the first Congress, honoring promises Federalists had tendered Anti-Federalists, did proceed in its first session to adopt the federal Bill of Rights. Ten out of seventeen proposed amendments were then ratified by the states, in recognition of the fact that people existed before governments, or as a delegate at the North Carolina convention, William Goudy, put it, "Power belongs originally to the people." The Federalists had contributed a workable form and structure of government at the Constitutional Convention; the Anti-Federalists had lent that structure perspective and honesty, in that the document did not take effect without safeguards for the people.

Thus it was that the new federal government came into being and set up business in the spring of 1789 in its temporary capital, New York City. In 1793 the government moved to Philadelphia, where Washington was inaugurated for the second time as president. That summer Philadelphians and Federalists suffered the visitation of a plague that is described in the following chapter.

THE PESTILENCE IN PHILADELPHIA

In Philadelphia, the second temporary capital of the new nation, the year 1793 began with no premonition of catastrophe. Early in January the whole town turned out to behold a great wonder. From the yard of the Walnut Street jail, a man took to the air. François Blanchard mounted in a balloon and remained aloft nearly an hour.

A distinguished Philadelphia physician, Dr. Benjamin Rush, enthusiastically reported the import of this event to a friend.

It was truly a sublime sight. Every faculty of the mind was seized, expanded and captivated by it. Forty thousand people concentrating their eyes and thoughts at the same instant upon the same object, and all deriving nearly the same degree of pleasure from it, added greatly to the novelty and originality of the scene. I cannot think that an invention in which so much ingenuity and fortitude have been displayed was intended only to amuse. . . .

The first command to man to "subdue" the earth like every other divine command must be fulfilled. The earth certainly includes water and air as well as dry land. The first and last have long ago yielded to the dominion of man. It remains for him only to render the air subservient to his will. This I conceive will sooner or later be effected by the improvement and extension of the principles of balloons. . . .

Perhaps they may carry astronomy so far beyond the gross air which lies near our globe as to enable them to make immense discoveries of the nature and number of the heavenly bodies. Perhaps they may facilitate the connection between distant countries by means of commerce. . . .

A pity, thought Rush, that his old friend Benjamin Franklin could not share this experience, but Franklin had died three years earlier. Rush's interests were nearly as manifold as Franklin's. He was a humanitarian working for the abolition of both slavery and capital punishment. During the Revolutionary War, when he had served briefly on the medical staff, he had striven mightily and loudly to reform the appalling conditions he had found in army hospitals. His gifts, some said, did not include tact; a misunderstanding with Washington himself had driven him back to his private practice, his enormously popular university lectures, and his work at the hospital. As physician he was soon to face the challenge of his life.

Philadelphia was well supplied with doctors, as the back country was not. In sickness country folk resorted to home remedies, sometimes adopted from their Indian neighbors, or relied upon the services of anyone laying a claim to medical knowledge. With no system of licensing, some of these "healers" were extraordinary, such as one charlatan a French traveler ran into near Lancaster:

Blanchard's famous balloon ascent; from a contemporary almanac.

Loaded with little bottles, he makes everyone he meets believe he is a doctor, sells his drugs, bleeds, pulls teeth, or
sells songs to those who don't want any of his medicine.
He has already bought from his profits a horse that carries
his pack, his dog, and himself. He stops at farms willing
to receive him (and many do in the name of science) eats
well everywhere, is gay, and seems to be a droll and crafty
rogue. He began life in Germany as a comedian.

Charlatanry was not unknown in Philadelphia, especially among the poor, but Dr. Rush, who had gone to
Edinburgh, Scotland, for his medical training, was one of
some eighty physicians practicing in the city. Six served
in rotation without pay to care for the patients in the
Philadelphia hospital "for the indigent, sick and insane."
Rush, perhaps the first American psychiatrist, took special
interest in the insane, taking them from their basement
(which Brissot had wondered about) to enjoy fresh air on
the grounds, collecting case histories, and introducing a
sort of occupational therapy.

When Schoepf had visited the hospital ten years earlier,
he had found only one wing completed. "There are only
two sick rooms, one for the women above, and one for the
men below. These rooms are high, airy, and large, and kept
like the whole establishment in a very cleanly state."
Schoepf had also made mention of quarantine and medical
inspection of incoming ships at Philadelphia's wharves:

The greed of the skippers often tempted them to stopple
too many passengers together, thus giving cause for dangerous maladies whereby many of these poor people were
done for without ever seeing the land for which, in the

hope of better fortune, they had given up home. . . . On several occasions ships had come to port with so much malignant tinder stowed . . . that no one could have stayed aboard 24 hours without falling a sacrifice. . . . No person was allowed on land until he had first been cleansed and all his old clothes thrown away, and then those landing were sent to an isolated spot on shore for a short quarantine.

Contagious diseases are exceedingly rare in America. In the country the people live scattered among shade trees; in the towns there is no crowding, almost every family living in its own home and everything clean.

Had the observant German revisited Philadelphia a decade later, he would have found disease. In spite of medical inspection, "malignant tinder" had come in, and by August 1793 it was a city of pestilence.

The immigrants who brought it were French, fleeing the terror of a slave rebellion—such as Jefferson had feared for America—in Santo Domingo. It had begun when the French Assembly, the government mounted by France's own revolution, reversed an earlier decree freeing the slaves on France's island colony. The slaves then rose in bloody revolution against their masters. Some of these reached Philadelphia penniless; a few managed to bring some of their slaves with them.

The only visible infection the refugees bore was influenza. It caused an epidemic, troublesome but not unduly alarming. But invisibly they brought worse. Yellow fever was common in Santo Domingo, and less malignant there than elsewhere; those who recovered from mild cases

Dr. Benjamin Rush by Thomas Sully.

enjoyed immunity. But the infection remained for a time in their bloodstream, to be extracted by any questing mosquito and carried to its next prey.

Some years later, Dr. Rush wrote a medical *Account of the Bilious Remitting Yellow Fever as it appeared in the City of Philadelphia in 1793*, as he struggled to understand its causes and effects. During what was shortly to become an epidemic, he carried on his usual correspondence with wife and friends.

In 1793 Philadelphia was having a hot and uncommonly dry summer.

There was something in the heat and drought of the summer months [read the Account], *which was uncommon, in their influence upon the human body. Labourers everywhere gave out (to use the country phrase) in harvest, and frequently too when the mercury in Fahrenheit's thermometer was under 84°. It was ascribed by the country people to the calmness of the weather, which left the sweat produced by the heat and labor, to dry slowly upon the body.*

Meanwhile, mosquitoes rose in swarms from the drying streams. Dr. Rush noted that the patients he treated for what at first he called "bilious remitting fever" often had inflamed mosquito bites. But even when he recognized the affliction as the dreaded yellow fever, he did not connect cause and effect.

The discovery of the malignity—extent—and origin of a fever which I knew to be highly contagious, as well as mortal, gave me great pain. I did not hesitate to name it, the Bilious Remitting Yellow Fever. . . . A hard trotting horse brought it on in two of my patients. . . . A supper of 12 oysters in one, and only 3, in another of my patients produced the disease.

More than a century would pass before the (Aedes aegyptes) mosquito's role in such epidemics was discovered.

Rush did not connect the epidemic with the coming of the French refugees, few of whom took the fever, which first appeared in homes along Water Street in early August. This street touched the waterfront, and however strict city officials were in enforcing quarantine, they had not put a stop to the unsanitary practice of shipowners who dumped their rubbish on the wharves. When later Rush searched to explain the disease, he wrote,

Cabbages, onions, black pepper, and even the mild potatoe, when in a state of putrefaction, have all been the remote causes of malignant fevers. The noxious quality of the effluvia from mill-ponds, is derived wholly from a mixture of the putrefied leaves and bark of trees, with water.

Rush wrote to his wife, who was spending the summer with relatives in New Jersey, about what had happened:

A malignant fever has broken out in Water Street between Arch and Race Streets, which has already carried off twelve persons. . . . It is supposed to have been produced by some damaged coffee which had putrefied on one of the wharves near the middle of the above district. The disease is violent and of short duration. In one case it killed in twelve hours, and in no case has it lasted more than four days. . . .

As yet it has not spread through any parts of the city

which are beyond the reach of the putrid exhalation which first produced it. *If it should, I shall give you notice that you remain where you are.*

Julia Rush, who had her younger children with her, was not to see Philadelphia again until mid-November. In the meantime two older sons, who had remained in the city, "discovered so much apprehension of being infected by my clothes" that Rush sent them to join her. Almost daily he wrote Julia, and to her his letters became a history of the pestilence:

August 25. The fever has assumed a most alarming appearance. It not only mocks in most instances the power of medicine, but it has spread through several parts of the city. . . . This morning I witnessed a scene . . . which reminded me of the histories I had read of the plague. In one house I lost two patients last night—a respectable young merchant and his only child. His wife is frantic this evening with grief. . . .

But in the *Account* he wrote,

Upon entering a sick room where a patient was confined by this fever, the first thing that struck the eye of a physician was the countenance. It was as much unlike that which is exhibited in a common bilious fever, as the face of a wild, is unlike the face of a mild domestic animal. The eyes were sad, weary, and so enflamed in some cases as to resemble two balls of fire. Sometimes they had a most brilliant or ferocious appearance. The face was suffused with blood, or of a dusky color, and the whole countenance was downcast.

Dr. RUSH's Directions *for the* Treatment *of the* bilious, inflammatory, remitting and intermitting YELLOW FEVER.

THE Symptoms of the first stage of this Fever are, chillinefs, head-ach, a flushing in the face, thirst, a red or yellow eye, with a dilated pupil, a quick, full, tenfe, low, flow, chorded, or intermitting pulfe—great pains in the back and limbs, frequent fighing, oppreffion at the breast, faintinefs, fleeplinefs, or delirium, a coftive, or a lax ftate of the bowels. Sicknefs and vomiting attend in many cafes.

As foon as you are affected, lofe ten or twelve ounces of blood from the arm, and repeat the fame quantity once or twice a day, while great pain and fever, or the above mentioned ftates of the pulfe, continue.

Take one of the purging powders (which are compofed of fifteen grains of Jalap and ten of Calomel) every fix hours, in firup or molaffes, until you have four or five large dark coloured, or black ftools. The powder may be taken before bleeding when the fever comes on at night, or where a bleeder cannot be fpeedily procured.

The operation of the purging powder fhould be affifted by drinking freely of thin drink of any kind.

The bowels fhould be opened two or three times every day during the continuance of the fever, by means of caftor-oil, or purging falts, or one of the purging powders, or by glyfters compofed of half a pint of water, with a quarter of an ounce of glauber-falt, or a table fpoonful of common falt in it.

Drink plentifully of toaft and water, tamarinds or apple water, balm-tea, or barley-water.

Napkins dipped in cold water, and applied to the forehead, bowels, ftomach, and limbs, give great relief in pains of thofe parts.

Glyfters of cold water afford immediate relief in pains of the bowels.

When the vomiting does not yield to bleeding and purging, it is often relieved by taking a table-fpoonful of fweet milk every hour.

Blifters fhould be applied to the neck, head, and limbs, and poultices of garlic to the feet, if the diforder fhould continue after fufficient evacuations have been ufed.

Camomile or centaury tea, porter and water, and weak broth, may be taken in this ftate of the diforder.

After the difeafe is fubdued, the ftrength may be reftored by a diet of chicken, veal, or mutton broth, beef tea, boiled white meats, tea, coffee, chocolate, and bread and milk, with the fruits of the feafon.

The dofes of the powder, and the quantity of blood drawn, fhould be lefs than have been mentioned, for young people and children, according to their age.

Cool and frefh air fhould be admitted freely to the fick, their linen changed every day, and all offenfive matters removed as fpeedily as poffible.

The efficacy of the above remedies depends upon their being early applied.

To prevent infection, a temperate diet, confifting of broths, milk, vegetables and fruits of all kinds fhould be ufed, and the exciting caufes of unufual heat, cold, labor, and fatigue from every caufe, fhould be carefully avoided.

Dr. Rush's own account of how he treated the plague; from a Philadelphia almanac, 1796.

He continued his letter to Julia:

While I depend upon divine protection and feel that at present I live, move, and have my being . . . in God alone, I do not neglect to use every precaution. . . . I even strive to subdue my sympathy for my patients; otherwise I should sink under the accumulated loads of misery I am obliged to contemplate. You can recollect how much the loss of a single patient once a month used to afflict me. Judge then how I must feel in hearing every morning of the death of three or four. . . .

Again he wrote in the *Account*:

A deep yellow color appeared in many cases within a few minutes after death. In some, the skin becomes purple, and in others black. . . . In some the skin was as pale, as it is in persons who die of common fevers. A placid countenance was observed in most, resembling that which occurs in an easy or healthful sleep.

To Julia:

September 18. In riding through town I was often stopped by half a dozen people, all imploring me to visit a wife, a husband, a brother, or a child. Judge how I must have felt in tearing myself away from them, for I could only visit a certain number, and by undertaking more than I could attend, some I knew would die of neglect.

So great is the apprehension . . . that I have seldom visited a patient the first time without being met at the head of the stairs by some member of the family in tears. Good Mrs. Mease took me by the hand the first time I visited her son and was dumb for some time with fear and distress. Another lady . . . fell upon my neck and wept aloud for several minutes before she would let me enter her husband's room. . . .

The *Account* read, "Grief, after a while, descended below weeping, and I was struck in observing that many persons submitted to the loss of relations and friends, without shedding a tear, or manifesting any other of the common signs of grief."

To Julia:

Many die without nurses. Some perish from the want of a draught of water. Parents desert their children as soon as they are infected, and in every room you enter you see no person but a solitary black man or woman near the sick. Many people thrust their parents into the streets as soon as they complain of a headache. Two such exiles have taken sanctuary for half a day in our kitchen and shop.

Some of the "black persons" Rush mentioned were the nurses he had recruited through an appeal to the Negro population he had inserted in the *American Daily Advertiser* in late August: "A noble opportunity is now put into their hands of manifesting their gratitude to the inhabitants of that city which first planned their emancipation from slavery and have since given them so much protection and support as to place them, in position of civil and religious privileges, on a footing with themselves." This was prefaced by a quotation from a physician "that there is something very singular in the constitution of the Negro which renders them not liable to this fever."

A civic group known as the Free African Society met to consider this plea. Its members doubted, with good reason, that any peculiarity in their constitution made them immune. That theory had arisen from earlier epidemics, like that in Charleston in 1699, when the whites had been ravaged and the Negroes had escaped. But most Carolina Negroes were then fresh from Africa, where they had acquired immunity just as the newly arrived French had from living in fever-ridden Santo Domingo. Frenchmen long settled in Philadelphia were subject to the disease, and in spite of the name of their society, most Philadelphia Negroes were generations removed from Africa.

They were also of two minds as to how much gratitude they owed the city. Emancipation was not absolute but gradual. Masters who freed their slaves without waiting for the law to take effect did not always have noble motives. Some merely thus dodged the obligation of supporting their "people" in their unproductive old age. And as in other northern cities, freedmen often had great difficulty in earning a livelihood. Without training in the skilled crafts, without capital to set up in business (bankers seldom made loans to Negroes), they had a desperate time finding their way. The Free African Society had been founded to cope with this situation.

But if they owed little to Philadelphia, they owed Dr. Rush a great deal. He was one signer of the Declaration of Independence who meant every word of it. He visited the freedmen in sickness and asked no fee. Recently, he had helped raise funds for the African Methodist Church, and just as the epidemic started was an honored guest at its roof-raising. The notion of a separate Negro church

Richard Allen.

offended many, both Negro and white, but Rush appreciated the circumstances: without warning and most rudely, the Negro worshipers at St. George's Methodist had been interrupted at their prayers and ordered to the gallery.

The society accepted the challenge. Two members, Richard Allen (an ex-slave and future Methodist bishop) and Absalom Jones, were given instructions in bleeding and dosing to take the place of doctors who had died or fled the city. Allen also took on the heavy duty of finding a graveyard crew to bury the dead. Others agreed to serve as nurses at wages set at $6 a week. Some volunteers refused to accept anything. And, Absalom Jones wrote later, "We have found them in various situations, some laying on the floor, as bloody as if they had been dipped in it. . . ."

"I will not sell my life for money," said Caesar Crandall, and set out on duties which presently killed him. A young girl made a bargain with God, which happily He kept: "If I go for money God will see it and may make me take the disorder and die, but if I take no pay He may spare my life." An old woman, asked her price, said, "Only a dinner, master, on a cold day."

People fled the city in panic. Those who remained adopted strange precautions. To prevent the contagion from moving from one street to the next, they built bonfires at the intersections. When this practice was forbidden as both dangerous and useless, they turned to gunpowder, firing their muskets incessantly until that, too, was stopped. Then, as reported by a local newspaper publisher, Matthew Carey, they tried other remedies:

The smoke of tobacco being regarded as a preventative, many persons, even women and small boys, had segars almost constantly in their mouths. Others, placing full confidence in garlic, chewed it almost the whole day; some kept it in their pockets and shoes. . . . Many houses were scarcely a moment in the day free from the smell of gunpowder, burned tobacco, niter, sprinkled vinegar. . . .

The *Account* read: "Finding them all ineffectual, I attempted to rouse the system by wrapping the whole body agreeably to Dr. [David] Hume's practice, in blankets dipped in warm vinegar."

According to Matthew Carey:

Some of the churches were almost deserted, and others wholly closed. The coffee-house was shut up, as was the city library and most of the public offices. Three out of the four daily papers were discontinued. . . . Many devoted no small portion of their time to purifying, scouring, and whitewashing their rooms. Those who ventured abroad had handkerchiefs or sponges impregnated with vinegar or camphor at their noses, or smelling bottles full of thieves vinegar. Others carried pieces of tarred rope in their hands, or camphor bags tied round their necks.

The *Account* continued: "I used bark in all its usual forms of infusion, powder, and tincture. I joined wine, brandy, and aromatics with it."

Carey wrote:

People . . . hastily shifted their course at the sight of a hearse coming toward them. Many never walked on the footpath, but went into the middle of the street to avoid being infected by passing a house wherein people had

died. Acquaintances and friends avoided each other . . .
and only signified their regard by a cold nod. The old
custom of shaking hands fell into such general disuse that
many shrank back with affright at the offer of a hand. A
person with a crape or any appearance of mourning was
shunned like a viper. And many valued themselves highly
on the skill . . . with which they got to windward of every
person whom they met. . . .

The corpses of the most respectable citizens, even of
those who had not died of the epidemic, were carried to
the grave on the shafts of a chair, the horse driven by a
Negro, unattended by a friend or relation and without
any sort of ceremony.

Things fell apart in Philadelphia. The Pennsylvania
legislature assembled on schedule August 27, but adjourned September 5. It must have been the shortest session on record. The federal Congress was not due to sit
until December, but most federal officials were on hand,
including President Washington. It was his time to va-
cation at Mount Vernon, but under these circumstances
he was uncertain where his duty lay. The flight of prominent citizens was adding to the panic; those doctors and
ministers who fled would never live it down. Washington
tried to induce his wife, Martha, to go home without him.
When she refused, he called his coach and set off, planning to return within two weeks. It was late October before he saw the capital again.

The *Account* read: "Water-Street between Market and
Race Streets became a desert. . . . The hearses alone kept
up remembrance of the noise of carriages or carts in the
street."

Cold Blows the Wind

This is often considered one of the most beautiful laments in the English language.

nev – er had but one true love, And in

green – wood she lies slain, In the

green – wood she lies slain.

I'll do as much for my true love
As any young man may;
I'll sit and mourn on her grave
A twelve month and a day.

The twelve month and the day was past,
The ghost began to speak:
"What makes you sit all on my grave
And will not let me sleep?"

"One kiss from you, my own sweetheart,
One kiss from you I crave,
One kiss from your lily-white lips
And I will go from your grave."

"My lips are cold as clay sweetheart,
My breath is earthy strong,
And if you kiss my lily-white lips
Your time will not be long."

"Down in yonder grove sweetheart,
Where you and I would walk,
The finest flower that ever I saw
Is withered to a stalk.

The stalk is withered and dry, sweetheart,
And the flower will never return,
And since I lost my own sweetheart,
What can I do but mourn?"

"Mourn not for me my own true love,
Mourn not for me I pray;
So I must leave you and all the world
And turn into my grave."

Governor Thomas Mifflin had left without arranging that the funds voted for relief by the legislature be turned over to the city. So, late in August, Mayor Matthew Clarkson sought advice from the College of Physicians. They recommended a massive cleanup campaign, of the wharves, the marketplace, private latrines, and the establishment of "a large and airy hospital" for the afflicted. And: "Place a mark upon the door or window of such houses as have any infected persons in it."

They had also put a stop to the tolling of bells. The churches had been tolling for each parishioner who died. Philadelphia had always been a city of bells; now the tolling had become incessant, demoralizing both sick and well. But the deathly silence when the bells were stilled was almost worse.

The *Account* continued:

But I did not abandon a hope that the disease might yet be cured. I had long believed that good was commensurate with evil, and that there does not exist a disease for which the goodness of Providence has not provided a remedy. Under the impression of this belief, I applied myself with fresh ardor to the investigation of the disease before me. I ransacked my library, and pored over every book that treated of yellow fever.

The cleanup campaign was carried out and continued. (When at long last fugitives returned, they marveled at the spotlessness of the plague-ridden city.) But in the meantime the plague went on, gathering momentum; it would not reach its climax until mid-October when more than a hundred would die.

In vain [read the Account] *were changes in the moon expected to alter the state of the air. The light of the morning, mocked the hopes that were raised by a cloudy sky in the evening. The sun ceased to be viewed with pleasure. Hundreds sickened every day beneath the influence of its rays. . . .*

A meteor was seen at two o'clock in the morning on the twelfth of September. It fell between Third-Street and the Hospital, nearly in a line with Pine-Street. Moschetos (the usual attendants of a sickly autumn) were uncommonly numerous.

The need of that "large and airy hospital" was urgent, for the Philadelphia Hospital had not been planned as a pest house. It could not be used, nor could the House of Correction ("Bettering House") for the poor. In despair, the authorities turned to the circus arena where an equestrian, Rickets, had lately displayed his feats on horseback. Wrote publisher Carey:

Thither they sent seven persons afflicted with the malignant fever, where they lay in the open air for some time, and without any assistance. Of these, one crawled out on the commons, where he died at a distance from the houses. Two died in the circus, one of whom was seasonably removed; the other lay in a state of putrefaction owing to the difficulty of procuring a person to remove him. . . .

The inhabitants of the neighborhood of the circus took the alarm and threatened to burn or destroy it, unless

The Pennsylvania Hospital in Philadelphia at the time of the plague.

the sick were removed; and it is believed they would have actually carried their threats into execution had compliance been delayed a day longer.

It was then that the guardians of the poor thought of Bush Hill, an estate on the outskirts of town. Its owner, William Hamilton, was away; so they took over the mansion and moved into it the four surviving patients on the circus grounds. But for a time Bush Hill was little better than the circus, where, according to Carey.

The sick, the dying, and the dead were indiscriminately mingled together. . . .
No wonder then that a general dread of the place prevailed through the city, and that a removal to it was considered as the seal of death. . . . There were instances of sick persons locking their rooms and resisting every attempt to carry them away. At length the poor were so much afraid of being sent to Bush Hill that they would not acknowledge their illness until it was no longer possible to conceal it. . . . The fear of the contagion was so prevalent that as soon as anyone was taken ill, of any disorder whatever, an alarm was spread among the neighbors, and every effort was used to have the sick person hurried off to Bush Hill, to avoid spreading the disorder.

On September 10 Mayor Clarkson appealed for volunteers. He and his three overworked guardians of the poor were nearly all that remained of city government, and the problems were frightful. Patients were escaping from the carts that carried them to Bush Hill. Responsible working people faced starvation because their employers had shut up shop and fled. Nearly thirty volunteers responded to the mayor's call.

So many civic leaders had left that the mayor could have known few of the men who now formed a committee and became the real administrators of the city. These few included a wealthy French-born merchant, Stephen Girard; the publisher of the newspaper quoted, Matthew Carey; and one doctor, Peter Helm. The others were small shopkeepers and mechanics, an umbrella maker newly come from England, a music master, a cobbler, and a number of carpenters and cabinet makers. Most served faithfully, some at the cost of their lives. The young widow of the stricken music master was to become First Lady as Dolley Madison.

After a horrified inspection of Bush Hill, Stephen Girard and Dr. Peter Helm volunteered for the worst job of all—management of the place. They needed money to hire competent nurses and a matron, to clean and ventilate the rooms, to get beds and provisions. A loan of $1,500 to begin the work was obtained from the Bank of America (the bank, incidentally, had been the idea of Alexander Hamilton, whose interest in monetary affairs had by now led him to become the first Secretary of the Treasury), and Girard and Helm set to work.

They were tireless. Besides directing the hospital staff, Girard did not flinch from giving the humblest service to the patients. Until the fatal mid-October when the plague nearly doubled in strength, Bush Hill was nearly adequate to the need. Some patients were discharged as cured, and the poor no longer shunned the place.

Bush Hill, near Philadelphia; from a 1793 engraving.

Another emergency was the care of orphans. "Mama's asleep, don't wake her," one child begged Richard Allen when he visited a stricken home. There was no danger of waking the mother; all he could do was summon his burial crew and find a refuge for the heartbroken child and for others that he found wandering helplessly in the streets.

According to publisher Carey:

The Bettering House in which such helpless objects had usually been placed, was barred against them. . . . The deaths of their parents and protectors, which should have been the strongest recommendation to public charity, was the chief cause of their distress and their being shunned as a pestilence. The children of a family once in easy circumstances were found in a blacksmith's shop, squalid, dirty, and half starved, having been for a considerable time without even bread to eat. . . .

The evil early caught the attention of [Mayor Clarkson's] committee, and on the 19th of September they hired a house on Fifth Street in which they placed 13 children. The number increasing, they on the third of October procured the Loganian Library. . . . A further increase . . . rendered it necessary to build some additions to the library. . . . From the origin of the institution, 190 children have fallen under their care, of whom 16 are dead, and about 70 have been delivered to their relations or friends. There are instances of five and six children of a single family in the house.

Some help came from outside. New York raised $5,000 for its sister city. Boston sent money and provisions. But such aid never met the need, and most communities were chiefly interested in avoiding infection. Stage coaches from Philadelphia were stopped outside town and their passengers refused food or shelter; ships made to anchor outside the harbor. Mail from the city was handled by tongs and dipped in vinegar. The eminence of the fugitives made no difference. The recently appointed Secretary of War, Benjamin Knox, had to spend a month in New Jersey before he was allowed to pass through New York on his way to Rhode Island.

Dr. Rush, who had more private patients than he and his three apprentices could handle, never visited Bush Hill, and the treatment administered there by an able physician from Santo Domingo, Dr. Jean Deveze, was anathema to him. Rush had finally discovered what he believed was the one cure for yellow fever in a manuscript given him by Benjamin Franklin. It consisted of massive doses of jalap and calomel, powerful purgatives, in a ration known as Ten-and-Ten, supplemented, when the pulse was hard and heavy, with copious bleedings.

"Bloodletting when used early on the first day frequently strangled the disease in its birth," according to the *Account*. The 3rd, 5th and 7th days were mostly critical, and the disease generally terminated on one of them, in life or death. . . ."

He converted many of his colleagues to this "cure," but others denounced it, and the controversy drew letters to the *Federal Gazette*. So public a demonstration of disagreement among physicians was bound to demoralize the readers, but since each side felt the other was killing the patients, they would not be silenced.

No physician sacrificed more to the welfare of his patients than Dr. Rush, and none was more wrong-headed.

He was not strong, he was indeed consumptive, but he spared himself nothing. The *Account* read, "The fever had a malignancy, and an obstinacy which I had never before observed in any disease, and it spread with a rapidity and mortality, far beyond what it did in the year 1762. Heaven alone bore witness to the anguish of my soul in this awful situation."

He sent no bills; he was bankrupting himself in buying his famous Ten-and-Ten for the poor. But how anyone survived his ministrations is the amazement of modern science, particularly in the matter of bleeding. From one patient he took 80 ounces of blood; that the man recovered is a tribute to his constitution—and to his faith in his doctor.

Dr. Rush had two other misconceptions. He believed that the refugees from the West Indies had nothing to do with the epidemic, and that no other feverish ailment could exist along with yellow fever. He wrote to Julia,

We have but one, we cannot have but one fever in town. The contagion of the yellow fever, like Aaron's rod, swallows up all the seeds of all other diseases. We might as well talk of two suns or two moons shining upon our globe as of two different kinds of fevers now in our city. . . . To suppose that because the yellow fever is epidemic in the West Indies and because it seldom occurs in North America, that it can exist among us only by importation, is as absurd as to suppose that the hurricanes which are so common in the West Indies, and which occur here only once in twenty or thirty years are all imported from that country.

He was wrong on both counts. His insistence that yellow fever was of local origin caused resentment. If Congress believed that, it would not wait until 1800 to move out of Philadelphia. And as a matter of fact, when it was finally convened in December, President Washington, after much study of the Constitution, assembled it in Germantown.

Rush had promised to send for his wife if he were stricken. He was stricken twice and did not let her know. His first attack, probably not yellow fever in spite of his theory about Aaron's rod, was mild. When in October he fell almost fatally ill, he concealed the severity of the attack from Julia.

Though he still had faith in his cure, by now he knew it was not infallible. It had not saved his three apprentices and his devoted sister. (His aged mother would have none of his doses and his bleeding; she survived.) The fever had now reached its mortal climax. He would not have Julia in the city, and reassured her by managing to write almost daily. Did she detect something like delirium in his letters?

I dreamed that I saw you at a distance at a window in a house in Coates Alley uptown, with a countenance healthy and pleasant, without the least tincture of that sallow gloom which pervades the face of every Philadelphian. I made signs to you that I would first go home and prescribe for my patients, and that I would come to you in the evening. But ah, I awoke soon afterwards and that evening did not come.

I recollect now that we had an infant called by your name. She was pleasant and smiled in my face the morn-

ing we parted. How does she do? How many teeth has she got? . . . I view you all at a distance on a safe and pleasant shore with your eyestrings pained in looking at me, paddling towards you in a boat shattered and leaky by many storms.

Rush had prayed for rain, for cool weather. But the *Account* read:

The pastures were descient, or burnt up. There was a scarcity of autumnal fruits in the neighborhood of the city. But while vegetation drooped or died from the want of moisture in some places, it revived with preternatural vigor from unusual heat in others. Cherry-trees blossomed, and apple, pear, and plum-trees bore young fruit in several gardens in Trenton, thirty miles from Philadelphia, in the month of October.

A heavy shower in September, a light frost in October, brought no relief. Then came a heavy frost, and though deaths continued for a time, there were no new cases. Fugitives began to return. "Strike out from the list of deaths in your letters Jos. Harrison and Jonth. Penrose. Many people walk the street now who were said to be dead."

By November he was looking for a house to receive his wife and children. He would not have them in an "infected house," and besides, the landlord had raised his rent. Before the middle of the month, they were back, though he would not admit them to his own room. "Kiss Ben. But ah, who will kiss my dear Julia?"

The end of the epidemic redoubled the controversies

about Rush's drastic treatment. Secretary of the Treasury Hamilton joined it; he had taken the fever and recovered, either because his boyhood in the West Indies had given him a partial immunity, or because of his French doctor's milder treatment. The latter was Hamilton's view, and embittered by the attacks on him, Rush seriously considered leaving the city which he, mistakenly or not, had served more devotedly than any other.

The dead were numbered at more than 4,000. Since in the confusion the count was undependable, there may have been as many as a thousand more. Philadelphia, then a city of somewhat over 50,000, had literally been decimated. Said the *Account*, "The poor were the first victims of the fever. From the sudden interruption of business, they suffered for a while from poverty, as well as disease. . . . The contagion after the second week of September, spared no rank of citizen."

Rush wrote his history of the disaster, and so did the publisher Matthew Carey; indeed, Carey went on writing it for years, expanding and revising each edition. A contemptuous reference to the work of the Negro nurses, later corrected, impelled Richard Allen and Absalom Jones to write their own account of the work of the Free African Society, which aside from recruiting nurses, had gone into debt to support the "graveyard crew." These men, both born in slavery, learned their letters late and with difficulty, but they wrote the most touching story of all, published as A *Narrative of the Proceedings of the Black People During the Late Awful Calamity in Philadelphia During the Year in 1793*. Two striking impressions were:

A cheerful countenance was scarcely to be seen in the city for six weeks. I recollect once in entering the house of a poor man, to have met a child of two years that smiled in my face. I was strangely affected by the sight. ... at this time the dread that prevailed over people's minds was so general, that it was a rare instance to see one neighbor visit another, and even friends when they met in the streets were afraid of each other, much less would they admit into their houses the distressed orphan that had been where the sickness was; this extreme seemed in some instances to have the appearance of barbarity.

Philadelphia had not seen the last of the fever; it came again and again, and reached other cities in spite of their precautions. But it never again achieved the malignance of the terrible year of 1793.

It might have comforted Rush to know that even today doctors have found no specific cure for yellow fever. That it has almost disappeared from the Western world is due to no miracle drug but to a miracle of prevention: Walter Reed's discovery of the mosquito's role and the effectiveness of inoculation.

★ | **8** | ★

THE WHISKY REBELLION

One of Richard Henry Lee's predictions about the new Constitution was that it would give everyone a little less representation than they had before. The first Americans to understand what this meant in practice were farmers in the four westernmost counties of Pennsylvania: Washington, Westmoreland, Fayette, and Allegheny.

These four counties were fertile, forested, and rippled with small hills, the plateau west of the Allegheny Mountains. Until the close of the Revolution, all but Westmoreland County had been disputed territory between Virginia and Pennsylvania; Westmoreland, of course, had been disputed between Connecticut and Pennsylvania. But since Virginia sold homesteads for one tenth of the cost exacted by its neighbor, the southernmost counties had been settled mostly by Virginians, some so poor that they lacked even the frontiersman's first necessity: a gun or firepiece. They had only their axes to fend off the wolves from preying on their few sheep, goats, and hogs, or to arm themselves against threatened Indian attack.

With these axes they felled timber to build their cabins, stacking the trunks one on top of the other and daubing the cracks with mud. They made the clearings to plant Monongahela rye and corn. The crops they harvested with their own hands. There were, however, a few "gentleman farmers," especially in Westmoreland County, who hired laborers to help with the planting and reaping.

Even for the better provided, frontier life was rugged in settlements thinly scattered over an area roughly the size of Connecticut. The women spun cloth from flax and wool to clothe their families. They ladled dinner upon wooden plates whittled by their husbands, and since water had to be laboriously fetched from a spring or well in a bucket, they did little washing or bathing.

They brought their children into the world with the help of a midwife, if they were lucky enough to have one near, and raised them with no medical help at all beyond home remedies. The family diet was meager: pork, hominy, bread, cornmeal pancakes, supplemented sometimes by game shot by those lucky enough to possess guns. They rarely ate vegetables. They were subject to the agues and rheumatic complaints prevalent in the area, and were endangered by rattlesnakes. But children who survived these perils grew into rugged adults.

Many settlers were of Scots-Irish origin and adhered to a severe form of Presbyterianism. In the more settled communities they built churches of logs, and elsewhere sat on the ground or on roughhewn benches to hear an itinerant preacher. Their beliefs were as strict as those of the old Puritans; only the psalms of David were acceptable for congregational singing.

The hard-working frugality of their lives is suggested

Pioneer cabin, 1796.

by a piece published in the *Pittsburgh Gazette* in 1786 over the signature "A Farmer."

My parents were poor, and they put me at 12 years of age to a farmer, with whom I lived till I was 21; my master fitted me out with two stout suits of homespun, four pairs of stockings, four woollen shirts, and two pairs of shoes; this was my whole fortune at my setting out in the world, and I thought it a good one: at 22 I married me a wife, and a fine young working woman she was: we took a farm of 40 acres on rent, by industry we gained a-head fast; I paid my rent punctually & laid by money; in 10 years I was able to buy me a farm of 60 acres, on which I became my own tenant . . . about this time I married my oldest daughter to a clever lad, to whom I gave 100 acres of my out-land; this daughter had been a working dutiful child, and I fitted her out well, and to her mind, for I told her to take of the best of my wool and flax, and to spin herself gowns, coats, stockings and shifts; nay, I suffered her to buy some cotton and make into sheets, as I was determined to do well by her. . . .

In all, the farmers of the four western counties of Pennsylvania had a passable and possible life, yet there was little of luxury in it, and one of their problems was a shortage of cash. It had for long been a problem, not just since the Revolution, because of their geographical situation. While some rye, furs, skins could be floated away on flatboats on the Monongahela River (Washington County) or on the Youghiogheny (Westmoreland County), the best markets were eastward, especially

Philadelphia. In that direction the Alleghenies formed a rampart.

The farmers had solved their cash problem rather ingeniously Instead of the pack trains straining under bushels making their way on impossible roads through the mountain barrier, the Pennsylvanians converted their rye to whisky. A farmer might brew for five or six of his neighbors at a roughhewn stillhouse. This whisky —rye rendered more compact—could go over the mountains in the saddlebags of horses. Their cash "crop," then, was whisky.

A new tax bill, which passed the federal Congress sitting at Philadelphia in 1791, had threatened to jeopardize this basis of their economy. It had been proposed by Secretary of the Treasury Hamilton, in an effort that the federal government might *assume* and pay all of the war debt, not just the nation's but the states'. While anyone may be loath to undertake a debt not his own, Hamilton had good reason. It is perhaps a truism that a creditor will always follow with interest the fortunes of a man who owes him money; Hamilton was a nationalist, and now creditors' eyes would be focused on the nation. What irony there may have been was this: most of the war debt was owed to well-to-do American bankers and merchants; however, to get funds to pay interest on it, Hamilton had proposed a tax on home-brewed whisky. It looked as if the new federal government was going to meet its obligations, and the states', by taxing its poorer citizens to pay its wealthier ones. The bill would require that stills be visited by tax collectors, inspected, and a seven-cent tax would be imposed on each gallon of whisky brewed.

William Findley, who had been elected representative to the federal Congress from Westmoreland County naturally protested. It was not difficult to imagine the hardship the tax bill would work on his constituents. Brewing was universal in Westmoreland. Why, Findley wrote (in A *History of the Insurrection in the Four Westernmost Counties of Pennsylvania*), "In many parts of the country, you could scarcely get out of sight of the smoke of a still house."

Then there was the principle: these first few years the federal government had been supported by taxes that the wealthy chiefly paid, because up to now only imports, and these often luxuries, had been deemed taxable. One thought of the fine wines with which President Washington plied his guests at stately and proper dinners, or the coach in which he drove about Philadelphia. And, one recalled, had not the Revolution itself been fought in part over this matter of excise taxes, as they were called, when the British had levied them on the colonies?

Besides, western Pennsylvania knew excise taxes from the Old World, and hated them. Chiefly Scots-Irish in origin, these now-American citizens remembered the excise taxes laid on their forbears by the British king. They liked to sing a ballad (written in 1790 by the Scotsman Robert Burns) about the day the Devil whisked away the tax collector.

The Devil Came Fiddling Through the Town

Written by Scots poet Robert Burns, this tune was published in 1792 and quickly gained popularity in the United States.

The de-vil came fidd – lin' through the town, And danced a – way with the Ex – cise – man, And ev – ery wife — cries: "Old_____ man, I__ wish you luck of the prize, man!" The

2. We'll make our malt, and we'll brew our drink,
   We'll laugh, sing and rejoice, man,
   And many brave thanks to the fine black devil
   That's danced away with the Exciseman.

   chorus

3. There's threesome reels, there's foursome reels,
   There's hornpipes and strathspeys, man,
   But the one best dance ever came to the land,
   Was The devil's away with the Exciseman!

   chorus

Despite Representative Findley's objections, the excise bill had passed; and when next he returned to Westmoreland he had the difficult task of trying to reconcile his constituents to it. Indeed, he found he could not reconcile them; they seemed determined not to pay, nor would persuasion have any effect on them. Findley wrote:

Nor did I know of any person then in the country, that approved of or advocated it as a good law. . . . Many of the uninformed people, being told by the warm advocates of the Federal government, that after it was ratified, we would have no more excises, considered the excise law therefore as unconstitutional. . . . It is not easy to convince a people that a law, in their opinion unjust and oppressive in its operation, is at the same time constitutional.

The law's constitutionality was not so serious a problem as the rumors now spreading in the four counties about worse taxes to come. They went from Pittsburgh, from village to village, and from one cluster of farms to another. Wags had it that there was shortly to be a tax of one shilling on a coat, a dollar on your plow, a dollar if your wagon went to Philadelphia, and two dollars if you gave birth to a son. This was serious.

Western Pennsylvanians took it seriously, too, and began to organize to resist. They held mass meetings at Redstone and Pittsburgh where speakers addressed the crowds; then petitions were drawn up, much like those Shays's men had sent to government. The western Pennsylvanians pronounced the tax collectors, to be appointed and sent to them, as "inimical to the interest of the country." They consolidated in denying "all aid, support and comfort" to them, a promise they would keep in the coming months.

In Philadelphia, the recently appointed secretary of the treasury learned of the uproar, and made a counter pronouncement. He called the mass meetings "intemperate" and paid no further heed to them. Such a response was dismaying to Representative Findley, and he had something to say on the subject:

It is true it may be posed that popular meetings are often conducted with indiscretion, and have a tendency to promote licentiousness. This is admitted; but it does not therefore follow, that such meetings should be prohibited by law or denounced by government. Doing so would be reducing the people to mere machines, and subverting the very existence of liberty.

President Washington's feelings, at this early stage of

government, seemed to Findley to be that law was law, and must be obeyed. In any case, tax collectors began their appointed rounds in September 1791. It was expected that they would inspect stills, collect the taxes, and all go smoothly; but it did not happen so. The farmers, perhaps rightly feeling their government had been insensitive, and as well knowing they were far from Philadelphia and safe from punishment, greeted the tax collectors with violence. There were feathers on their turkeys, and they were well able to make tar, and so, reported Findley,

The first actual outrage was committed in September, 1791, on a Robert Johnson, collector of excise for Washington and Allegheny counties, by a party of armed men disguised. The attack was made on him near Pigeon creek. After cutting his hair, they tarred and feathered him, and in this situation compelled him to walk some distance.

The next act of violence was committed on a man of the name of Wilson, who was in some measure disordered in his intellects, and affected to be, perhaps thought he was, an excise-man, and was making enquiry for distillers. He was pursued by a party, taken out of his bed and carried several miles to a smith's shop; there they stripped off his clothes and burnt them, and burning him in several places with a hot iron, they tarred and feathered and in that situation dismissed him.

Soon some such parties of western Pennsylvania came to be called "Whisky Boys." They did not stop at tar and feathers, but warned their neighbors of dire consequences if they rented a house or room to a tax collector. When flouted, the Whisky Boys meted out punishment. In August 1792 a Captain Falkner was so unwise as to "let his house to the inspector to hold his office in." Findley reported the result:

> [Falkner] was attacked on the road by a person with a drawn knife, and threatened that his house should be burned for permitting an office of inspection to be held in it. He escaped, on giving a promise to prevent further use of his house for an office, and accordingly gave public notice in the newspapers, that the office should be no longer kept in his house.

Occasionally, there was an attempt to bring some of these parties to justice, but this was erratic. Findley did know of one such case, however, and of the failure of the attempt. A subpoena was being sent to the group of distillers who had attacked Robert Johnson, but the deputy marshal, perhaps timid himself, chose to send it "under cover as private letters, by a poor simple man, who had been usually employed in driving cattle, &c." According to A History,

> What better could the inspector expect? . . . The sheriff or constable will be respected when the officious bum will probably be well flogged, but in this instance the poor man was taken for a bum and treated accordingly, without knowing the nature of the service he was employed about. He was seized, whipped, tarred and feathered, and it is said that his money was taken from him, and finally, being blindfolded, he was tied in the woods, and remained in that situation for five hours.

In the next few years a few more incidents occurred.

Some barns and an inspector's house were burned; the mail between Philadelphia and Pittsburgh was robbed, probably in an attempt to intercept government orders; and a large crowd paraded through Pittsburgh. It was in all a peaceful parade, but nevertheless alarmed the small shipping town Forman had seen on his way to the Mississippi.

All this, like some of the details of Shays's Rebellion, was in approved revolutionary tradition, but Philadelphia no more approved of it than Boston had approved Shays. A year and a half passed; on September 15, 1792, President Washington issued a demand for law and order.

Within a year his proclamation had had little effect, while his government was on shaky footing elsewhere. It looked as if the new nation might become involved in a foreign war: American sailors had been kidnapped from their vessels by the belligerent powers, and the Spaniards had closed the Mississippi to American boatmen. Beset by many difficulties, perhaps Washington was more convinced than he ought to have been by a report Secretary Hamilton now delivered to him. It described what was happening in western Pennsylvania in exaggerated terms, or this was the belief of Findley, who had worried lest the president give it credence. Hamilton's report, Findley wrote,

begins with denouncing those people for holding and circulating opinions, which if they were criminal, had been entertained and circulated by the most respectable authority in the United States long before [no taxation without representation], and it goes on to enumerate the acts of opposition with the highest colouring they would possibly bear, and intermixes real facts with misrepresentation or even worse, and concludes in such a manner as to leave an impression that there was not a good citizen in that country but the excise officers.

Findley was shaken. He considered nothing that had happened in the western counties serious enough to justify the heat of Hamilton's report. "Even where a government is good in itself," he murmured, "it may be perverted in the administration." He did not understand how Hamilton and Washington could assume that everyone attending the mass meetings was a traitor, opposed to government. Findley had attended them himself, and saw there many other responsible citizens who had come in the hope of curbing the hotheads.

The latter had been present. One of them, who had masterminded the mail robbery, had uttered sedition. Findley wrote,

Like the spirit which at unlucky occasions actuated the Israelitish king, the frenzy which actuated [William] Bradford during the whole of this period . . . impelled him to rise and address the committee in a most extravagant language, in the course of which he urged erecting an independent government and alleged that the Federal government had only temporized with Spain and Britain about the western posts, and trifled with the Indians. Let us be independent, said he, and we will accomplish these objects in a few months. For a source of supplies he proposed killing the first army that came against us, and supplying ourselves with arms and ammunition.

Washington in Philadelphia had had enough, and a report of Bradford's speech only intensified his resolution

Militiaman says goodbye to his wife before marching away.

to quell what he had come to regard as a revolt in western Pennsylvania. As he told Findley later in conversation, he had begun to feel it "his duty to bring out such a force as would not only be sufficient to subdue the insurgents, if they made resistance, but to crush to atoms any opposition that might rise in any other corner." The president was not usually so harsh. What he had not heard was that Bradford had not carried the meeting at which he spoke; far wiser counsel had carried the day to such effect that Bradford fled and was heard no more.

Washington summoned the militia from Pennsylvania, New Jersey, Maryland, and Virginia on August 7, 1794. A month later, as pumpkins ripened, just under 16,000 troops were on the field heading for the mountains. It seemed an excessively large force to be sent against delinquent taxpayers, but the majesty of government was to be demonstrated. Infantry, cavalry, artillery, and light-horse dragoons moved in two flanks—the southern from Maryland and Virginia, the northern from Pennsylvania and New Jersey toward Parkinson's Ferry on the Monongahela and Budd's Ferry on the Youghiogheny River, where they would rendezvous. This was the heart of the disturbed district.

While the president did not accompany the troops this far, as commander in chief he initially led them, with Hamilton riding alongside as had been done during the Revolution. Hamilton had also drawn up instructions for the militia on the expedition, by which he hoped to make citizens obey the law. The expedition's goals were:

1st. To suppress the combinations which exist in some of the western counties of Pennsylvania in opposition to the laws laying duties upon spirits distilled within the United States, and upon stills.

2nd. To cause the laws to be executed.

These objectives are to be effected in two ways:

1. By military force.

2. By judiciary process and other civil proceedings.

The objectives of the military force are twofold:

1. To overcome any armed opposition which may exist.

2. To countenance and support the civil officers in the means of executing the laws.

However well directed and organized, to Representative Findley this force naturally looked like a vast and threatening mass of men being sent against civilians. He worried over their military airs, and seemed to feel the government had encouraged their martial aspect by incendiary recruiting posters. It had been difficult to fill the ranks, especially in Quaker Pennsylvania. Thus, Findley wrote, "It was necessary to address them with recruiting orations, calculated to rouse their passions. For this purpose, trifling incidents were magnified into crime and the most orderly civilians were characterized as offenders."

For the troops themselves, it was in some ways a fall outing, with drummers and fifers accompanying. They got to see Norristown, Reading, and Harrisburg, and encamped in meadows along the banks of the Schuylkill and Susquehanna rivers in pleasant weather. One of them, a twenty-four-year-old from New Jersey, was keeping a diary and we turn to him for a moment.

He was John Hugg Clunn of the quartermaster's department, and his journal records the buying of supplies —beef, cheese and bread, the straw used for bedding— and finding a stillyard—or scales—on which to weigh them. But first and last his real interest was girls.

Rose at Revelee beating, and the detachment was in motion a little after sunrise. . . . Rode on before the troops. After leaving them about two miles, overtook a young woman on horseback. Rode with her a mile, where the road forked and we parted. On looking back to see how she went, my Creature made a stumble, fell on her head, and away went I, I knew not where until I found myself almost covered with mud and my mare on my back.

This accident was not disabling: "I felt well but dirty." Two days later, in Reading on October 4, Clunn's duties gave him further opportunity for girl-watching.

Went to the Baker's for to hurry the Baking of the Bread. Found a pretty Girl there, the man's Daughter. Asked her to go over to the tavern to dance, which she would willingly have done, but her father set her at making Biscuit. She seemed to understand it and handled them with great dexterity.

The next day being Sunday, "dressed myself in Stile, Powdered hair and silk stockings" and went to church. On October 8 in Myerstown, he had a look at the canal under construction to link the Schuylkill and Susquehanna rivers, and met another girl in a very odd encounter.

Passing a fine house I stopped a moment to view it. A young woman in the door desired me to walk in, which I accordingly did and was placed by a fine fire. She appeared to be in great spirits and soon after informed me that her sister, the Gens. wife who owned the house lay dead. I laughed at her and would have she was punning, adduced as a reason the house being open, the shutters of the windows not closed, and she being in such a merry humor.

However my curiosity being somewhat excited . . . she led me into the room, and Ye Gods! There she lay. I cannot describe my feelings; they were distressed and I hurried away as soon as possible, though the girl made me promise to call on my return.

Here are some samples from the diary of another New Jerseyan, an older man. He was Captain David Ford, recording his encampment at Crooked Billet on a "very rough, bad piece of ground":

Towards evening the hemisphere began to thicken and looked like a heavy gust. . . . The whole heavens appeared in a blaze, and peals of thunder succeeded each other so rapidly as scarcely to afford an interval for several hours. A more tremendous thunderstorm I never saw.

Here again I was very much pleased with the . . . enterprise of my troops, who had all taken precaution of trenching around their tents, and when the storm began, they turned out with whips, which they had previously prepared, and whipped their tents; the effect of which is to wet them all as soon as possible, after which they leak no more. I did so with my own and laid myself down to perfect rest.

To return to Representative Findley. He feared that the rain, which continued, would begin to sour the temper of the troops. If Captain Ford seemed content and cheerful, nevertheless others, Findley contended, "filled the news-papers with complaints and sarcasms on the whisky-men."

It was perhaps only to be expected, and by now rumors of such restlessness in the militia were reaching the west. In response to them, and to the vast size of the federal army, many who had sympathized with the Whisky Boys repented their rashness. On September 24, another large meeting was held at Parkinson's Ferry. Western Pennsylvanians drew up a petition with many signatures pledging submission to the federal law. The gathering asked Findley to bear their petition to Washington, now approaching Carlisle, and persuade the president to turn the troops back.

By early October 6,000 troops were encamped on the common at Carlisle, and Washington, Findley, Ford, and Clunn all arrived in town within a few days of each other. Carlisle was, like Pittsburgh, something of a shipping station for western commerce, and with tanner's and glassmaker's establishments. When the president arrived, a cannonade was fired to greet him, church bells were rung. But the crowd that gathered in the streets to watch him pass was strangely silent.

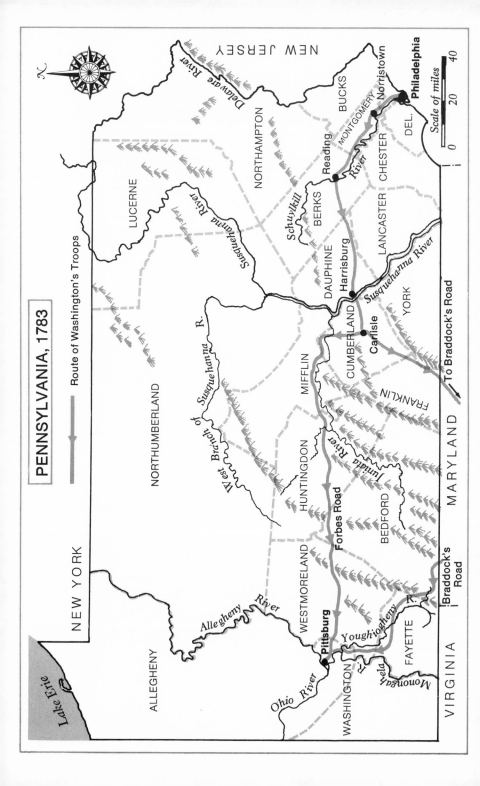

PENNSYLVANIA, 1783

Route of Washington's Troops

Scale of miles
0   20   40

NEW YORK

Lake Erie

ALLEGHENY

NORTHUMBERLAND

LUCERNE

West Branch of Susquehanna R.

Susquehanna River

NORTHAMPTON

Delaware River

NEW JERSEY

BUCKS

MONTGOMERY

Norristown

Philadelphia

DEL.

Reading

BERKS

Schuylkill

Schuylkill River

DAUPHINE

Harrisburg

LANCASTER

CHESTER

Susquehanna River

YORK

MIFFLIN

CUMBERLAND

Carlisle

FRANKLIN

To Braddock's Road

HUNTINGDON

Juniata River

MARYLAND

Forbes Road

BEDFORD

WESTMORELAND

Allegheny River

Pittsburg

Ohio River

Youghiogheny R.

Monongahela R.

WASHINGTON

FAYETTE

Braddock's Road

VIRGINIA

Clunn's attention was on the tavern.

I saw several good looking girls. Betsy Davis at the tavern was somewhat handsome, though very young and bashful. Fell into a milch [milk] punch club who were very lively. About 11 o'clock moved for visiting the Colonel with a flute and violin and form a serenade. . . . On our arrival played a march, huzzaed, went in and was treated with kindness and rack punch. Returned in disorder, felt chagrined. They broke a chair, overset a large table.

Captain Ford, in an approving manner, noted in his diary that a few prisoners had been taken. One of them was

an Irish schoolmaster, who had been a very busy fellow in the way of sedition; he was very much frightened when taken; he had repeatedly said, he would himself blow the president's brains out if he attempted to lead the army over the mountains against the insurgents and much like talk; he was committed to jail.

Representative Findley reached Carlisle on October 10, and had first impressions of the town that alarmed him. "The streets and avenues," he wrote, ". . . were occupied by the army, during the night, . . . apprehension of the town being burnt excited a general panic." He learned that fifty of the militia had been dismissed for pilfering, which seemed to confirm his suspicions that the troops had become licentious. Nor were his fears allayed by a talk with a colonel from Pennsylvania, who colorfully expostulated that were a Whisky Boy met with, he "would be skewered, shot or hanged on the first tree."

There had also been two deaths, whose accounts Findley gave:

Two men had been killed, one on the great road near Lebanon, and the other at a house in the neighborhood of Carlisle. The one on the road was killed by the Jersey troops. He provoked an officer by foolish and insulting language, and on laying hold on one of the bayonets of the guard, who were ordered to arrest him, he was run through the body. He was evidently drunk or deranged. Surely so many men in arms could easily have secured one unarmed fool, without killing him.

The other death had been a boy

killed by a light horseman from Philadelphia, who went into the country to seize some persons who had assisted at erecting liberty poles in Carlisle. The young man, who was killed, was not only innocent, but very unwell. The party left him under guard of one of their number, until they would search the bar for others. The sick boy declaring his innocence, that he was not able to stand, attempted to go into the house without leave; the light horseman ordered him to stop, on the peril of being shot, and if he could not stand, to sit or lay down, and in the mean time cocked his pistol. When the boy was in the posture of laying himself down, and the light horseman about to uncock his pistol, it went off . . .

The second killing had been accidental, but Findley feared other accidents if the army marched across the mountains. He went to call on the president. Washington greeted him, he wrote, "with that candour and politeness which have at all times distinguished his character." Then their negotiations began. Assuring the president that the westerners were reconciled to peace and would comply with federal law, the representative presented the petition.

President Washington responded by being perfectly polite, but quite inconclusive. On the one hand, "he authorized us to assure the citizens who had sheltered themselves under the faith of government, that no hair of their head should be injured, let their crimes have been ever so great." Yet quite contradictorily, during these same negotiations,

he . . . pressed it on us to take the utmost care that one gun should not be fired, and added that if one gun was fired, he would not be responsible for the consequences; we assured him there was no design of making resistance, but on the caution being repeated, we remarked that if a fool or desperate man, to prevent himself from being taken, should fire a gun, that it would be a great hardship if the whole country should be implicated in his guilt; he [Washington] answered that he did not intend that they should, but that we did not know what might be the consequence of firing one gun.

The president seemed to have taken refuge in a cloud of promises, while it became clear that the troops would not be turned back. On this point Washington was unshakable, giving as his reason that the expedition had already cost far too much for withdrawal.

He appealed to our own knowledge, that the preparation

General Washington reviews his troops at Fort Cumberland, October 18, 1794.

*for the expedition was the greatest part of the expence,
and observed, that being thus far advanced, it would be
necessary to obtain further and more ample assurances
of submission, before he could dismiss the army, than
perhaps would have been required at an earlier period.*

Washington refused to countermand the march. He
left to review the militia from Virginia and Maryland
before returning to Philadelphia, leaving General Henry
Lee (and the disturbingly ubiquitous Hamilton) to lead
the troops toward the Alleghenies.

As they neared the foothills of the mountains at the
end of October, the soldiers were beginning the first
seriously rugged part of their journey. Only a scattering
of roads could be taken through these ridges. The northern flank went on Forbes Road, once an Indian trail and
running alongside the waters of the Juniata River. Braddock's Road was the route of the southern flank, a
French and Indian army road, built then, but by now
unclear and overgrown.

The beauty of the mountains was impressive as the
autumn rainfalls continued, but the roads suffered.
"Such roads were never known (with me)," Quartermaster Clunn confessed,

*There was nothing but rocks first, and then mud almost
middle deep, yet with all these inconveniences they
marched 16 miles [one day]. Only two companies baggage came forward, and near 5,000 troops lay in damp
fields, mostly meadow, without any covering save the
Heavens during an incessant rain which continued all
night.*

I really felt for them, though it was with much difficulty that I produced a berth for myself, which was in a tent with eight companions. If it had not been for whiskey many a poor fellow would have given up. They were somewhat elevated, and seemed to pass the night . . . very agreeably. Large fires were built, and there was singing in all quarters.

Oct. 27th. Orders were issued for the troops to tarry this day and an extraordinary ration of whiskey to be issued. About 12 o'clock the tents arrived and the whole were satisfied.

Did the "extraordinary ration" come from the mountain distilleries? Hamilton, who was somewhere along the line of march, had recommended its purchase, from registered distillers naturally, for the use of the army whenever possible.

Clunn still had to forage the country, here seizing a wagonload of straw, here six horses to transport ordnance. "It is a disagreeable act to a person of tender and humane feelings, but we were in a starving condition, our provisions out, and none within eight miles, therefore necessity, which has no law, impelled us in it."

In the "rebel" counties, requisitioning of supplies was the nearest Clunn's outfit came to military action. He had leisure to write his sister Peggy, to go sight-seeing at Braddock's Field and Pittsburgh. There he saw some of the Whisky Boys brought in, but only as an observer: "The light troops arrived here from the other side of the Monongahela with sixty prisoners," he wrote. "In Gnl. B. Brigade we have about fifty prisoners. What will be their fate we know not. The part of the town that fronts the river is pleasantly situated."

It is a pity that Clunn lacked the curiosity to inquire into the arrest of the prisoners he saw brought into Pittsburgh. One would like to check against the account written by Representative Findley. Yes, the militia had rendezvoused at Budd's and Parkinson's ferries, muddy places. But there had been a full snowstorm on November 13 when the generals ordered militia companies out to take prisoners in the four counties. The seizures were done at night, and the inhabitants of Washington County gave it the name of "dreadful night."

Some were taken decently, but in other cases the militia, appearing unexpectedly, spent the night dragging unprepared men from their wives and children. Findley claimed that the prisoners to be next mentioned, were taken from two lists handed General William Irvine, one a list of suspects, one of witnesses against them, with no indication of which was which. The general grabbed them all.

A number of citizens were dragged out of their beds in the night and marched to the camp with scarce sufficient time to put on their necessary clothing. The camp affording no better accommodations, they were obliged to lay that night on the wet earth under snow and rain, and to add to their misery, they complain that they were barbarously insulted . . . contrary to the orders of the general.

Findley described other arrests:

A captain with a detachment of the army who took a number of prisoners in the southern parts of Washington [County] is asserted to have driven the prisoners . . . like cattle at a trot through muddy roads and through creeks up to their middle in water, and to have impounded them in a wet stable at night. . . .

On Thursday, the 13th November, there were about forty persons brought to Parkinson's house by order of General White; he directed to put the damned rascals in the cellar, and to tie them back to back, to make a fire for the guard, but to put the prisoners back to the farther end of the cellar, and to give them neither victuals nor drink. The cellar was wet and muddy, and the night cold; the cellar extended the whole length under a large new log house, which was neither floored, nor the openings between the logs daubed. They were kept there until Saturday morning, and then marched to the town of Washington. On the march, one of the prisoners who was subject to convulsions [epilepsy?], fell into a fit; but when some of the troop told general White of his situation, he ordered them to tie the damned rascal to a horse's tail, and drag him along with them, for he had only feigned having the fits. . . . This march was about twelve miles. The poor man, who had the fits, had been in the American service during almost the whole of the war with Great Britain.

Findley had no admiration at all for Secretary Hamilton, whom he charged with sole responsibility "for the violent crisis that took place." Here is his somewhat prejudiced account:

When the President returned to Philadelphia [from Carlisle] the Secretary of the Treasury remained, and marched with the right wing of the army, and . . . was extremely attentive to [its wants] and was looked up to

by many in it as something even more than the com-
mander-in-chief. *The superb marquee which he occupied,
and which was by far more extensive and elegant than
that of the commander . . . contributed to draw the attention of the army and of the country people to him
as a man of more than common authority. . . .*

*It is well known . . . that orders were sometimes issued
by him, and that he considered no officer in the army as
beyond his control. . . . To him has been ascribed by
some in the army the measure of discipline that was
preserved in it and the regularity of the supplies they
received, though this was undoubtedly ascribing too
much to him.*

Findley was particularly annoyed by the part Hamilton
played in the hearings of those arrested to determine if
their guilt justified their being sent to Philadelphia for
formal trial. In demanding a confession, Hamilton had
a way of saying that evasion was useless, since he knew
everything already. Such, to Findley's wrath, was his
manner with a sheriff who had done his utmost to keep
order in the country.

Of hundreds arrested, only twenty prisoners, two of
them from Virginia, were brought to Philadelphia for
trial. They reached there on Christmas Day, and were
paraded through town with slips of paper marked "In-
surgent" in their caps.

Only two were condemned for treason, and these were
later pardoned by Washington. One man died in jail,
poor old Herman Husband, who had often entertained
visitors to his mountain home with his odd theories of

American geography based on his interpretation of the prophecies of Ezekiel.

For an expedition involving so much sound and fury, this was a strangely meager result. The more long-range injury was suffered not by those arrested, but by other leaders in the western counties, who remained under suspicion for years. One of these was Findley, who wrote his book to clear his name (and becloud Hamilton's).

I say when these circumstances are candidly reflected on, the reader will be able to decide for himself, whether there is not . . . solid ground . . . to conclude that the Secretary himself at this period contemplated and planned to promote the violent crisis that took place. By his own account we find he was regularly informed by his spies of the most minute circumstances of the clandestine outrages, and conducted his plan in a manner best calculated to excite an open rupture. If this was not his design, why did he not use the proper means of restraining offenses in season?

This accusation was going too far. From the number of the innocent of whom the secretary of the treasury claimed guilty knowledge, it is obvious that his "spies" had not always informed him accurately. His joining the military expedition has a simple explanation: his sword was jealous of his mightier pen. He was dissatisfied with the part he had played in the Revolution, honorable though it was; he was an admirer of the military achievements of young Napoleon Bonaparte. The Whisky Rebellion, as the government called it, offered him a chance for real military distinction.

As for John Hugg Clunn, by mid-December he was back in New Jersey, carrying with him an apple, a "dear pledge of a female's offered friendship" from yet another girl he met on the way, and suffering from a sense of anticlimax over his soldierly accomplishments.

Thus ended a Campaign (if it maybe so called) of near three months without action. Yet I verily believe we had hardships and troubles to overbalance, as I feel firmly persuaded our troops would rather have encountered an army of disciplined [men] equal in number to themselves and trusted to the issue, which is the honor of our countrymen . . . rather than have encountered the hardships we have all undergone. It was bad, visibly unaccountable, and what few armies before have ever accomplished in so short a time, even with the shedding of blood—suppressing an insurrection in their country.

If Clunn sounds confused, he was not alone. About it all, Representative Findley seems to have turned from activist to philosopher. He wrote, "While things were in this state, I have heard men talk as if they were all Samsons, who each could kill his thousands with the jawbone of an ass."

Critics would claim that the government had by its own stupidity created what it called the Whisky Rebellion. For this it would pay heavily. Washington's government had lost popularity, and a day of reckoning would come in the election of 1800.

★ 9 ★

THE LYON OF VERMONT

In 1793 events across the Atlantic captured the fancy and roused the passions of many Americans. England and France were at war, and Americans promptly took sides.

Who but a Tory, asked some, would side with England, so recently an enemy, a wicked stepmother to her former colonies? What patriot would not defend France, friend in need during the Revolution, and home of their benefactor, young Lafayette? The choice, however, was not as simple as that.

Intense interest in European affairs had begun in 1789 when the French exploded into revolution against their monarchy. At this stage it was a revolution after the hearts of many Americans, and in the image of their own. Did not Lafayette support it?

But even then there were doubters, and the worst fears of these were confirmed when the so-called Reign of Terror began in France. In 1793 the French king went to the guillotine, and after him much of the nobility. Lafayette would have been among them had he not been captured by the Austrians. Revolutionary France became involved in a bloody struggle with the other European powers, and Americans were divided. The result was the crystallizing of two political parties, the Republicans and the Federalists.

The Republicans supported the French Revolution. The party, led by Thomas Jefferson, found its support mainly in the rural West and South. Included among Republicans were frontiersmen, farmers, and small townspeople who shared Jefferson's skepticism about cities, industrialization, and high finance. In this foreign war, the Republicans, then, wished to side with France, not with colonialist England.

Opposing them, the Federalists, including Alexander Hamilton, favored Great Britain in this foreign war. Few of the framers of the Constitution had believed in the innate goodness of the common man. Often aristocrats themselves, they assumed the "best" people would rule, that is, a tiny minority.

Even more, the Federalists had been alarmed by the fate of the French aristocrats when the French Revolution entered its bloody phase. Would this be their fate in America, if the American people ever became aroused? In the ranks of Federalists could be found many framers of the Constitution, the Northeast establishment, and many merchants afraid of losing trade with England by declaring war on her. Certainly shipowners felt this way.

Thus polarization set in and the quality of the American political scene in the 1790s deteriorated rapidly, at least as reflected by its press. Having taken sides, some editors harangued like fishwives; some contributors sent scurrilous exaggerations for publication.

One of the most vociferous Republican editors was Benjamin Franklin Bache, grandson to Franklin but as hotheaded as his grandfather had been cautious. Bache's sheet, the *Aurora*, exclaimed, "What a glorious period will that be when all king-craft, priest-craft, feudal rights, monarchies, aristocracies and all other tyrannies shall be swept from the face of the earth." The *Aurora* also mentioned an attempt to assassinate George III of England, lauding the attempt though it had failed: someone had fired a musket at the king when he was riding in his carriage.

But the *Aurora* had no praise at all for President Washington, naturally regarded as the head of the Federalist party since he was president. Washington, as will be seen, had little wish to align himself with either side. But viewing him as if he did, the *Aurora* described such victories as he had won during the Revolution as "microscopic." In these pages Washington read that he had dragged out the war without reason; and as he was preparing to retire from the presidency in 1795, he read this:

The flattery, nay the adoration that has been heaped upon him, has made him forget that he is a mortal, and he has been persuaded to believe, and his actions squint that way, that like Alexander he is an immediate offspring of the gods. . . . If ever a nation was debauched by a man, the American nation has been debauched by Washington. . . . If ever a nation was deceived by a man, the American nation has been deceived by Washington. Let his conduct then be an example to future ages. Let it serve to be a warning that no man may be an idol and that a people may confide in themselves rather than in an individual. . . .

*If ever there was a period of rejoicing, this is the mo-
ment—every heart, in unison with the freedom and happiness of the people ought to beat high with exultation
that the name of* WASHINGTON *from this day ceases to
give currency to political iniquity and to legalize corruption.*

Reacting to events in France, Federalists high in government, in their turn, seemed to see a bloodthirsty
revolutionary behind every bush. "Jacobin emissaries,"
wrote one senator,

*are sent to every class of men, and even to every indi-
vidual man that can be gained. Every threshing floor,
every husking, every party at work on a house frame or
raising a building . . . the very funerals are infected with
brawlers and whisperers against government.*

Such an impression had of course been contributed to
by those Federalist editors who had also taken sides. One
was William Cobbett, also known as Peter Porcupine,
presumably because his remarks stung. In an issue of his
Gazette, published in Philadelphia where the *Aurora* also
appeared, he printed a wild article under the auspices of
warning his countrymen about "Cruelty the National
Character of the French." "At this time of public alarm
and consternation," went the article, the following account should be "engraved on the memory of every father and mother who reads it, and be related by them
over and over, till their children learn it by heart." What
he wanted memorized was this:

At Nantes [France] they hung up several women and

The Bastille.

maids by their feet, and others by their arm pits, and thus
exposed them to the public view stark naked.

Some they bound before a great fire, and being half
roasted let them go; a punishment worse than death.

Amidst a thousand hideous cries, and a thousand blas-
phemies, they hung up men and women by the hair, and
some by their feet—on hooks in chimnies, and smoked
them with wisps of wet hay till they were suffocated. . . .

They stripped them naked, and, after a thousand in-
dignities stuck them with pins and needles from head to
foot. They cut and slashed them with knives and, sometimes with red hot pincers took hold of them by the
nose, and other parts of the body, and dragged them
about the room.

In some places they tied fathers and husbands to their
bedposts, and before their eyes ravished their wives and
daughters with impunity. They blew up men and women
with bellows till they burst them.

Naive readers must have marveled at Peter Porcupine's
ability to get so timely an account of events in France.
Only a rare scholar recognized that the report was based
on allegations following a religious massacre a century
earlier. The Porcupine could count on their rarity. "I say
beware," he wrote, "ye understrapping cuthroats who
walk in rags amidst filth and vermin, for if once the
halter gets around your flea bitten neck, howling and con-
fessing will come too late."

In spite of such "yellow journalism," not all of the
American press of the day followed suit. In addition to
such scurrilous trash many papers published long, closely
reasoned pieces by public-spirited citizens on the order of
the famous *Federalist Papers*.

However, the extremists had alarmed and disgusted George Washington. When in 1796 he retired at the end of his second term as president, he took the occasion of his farewell address to warn Americans against the rash party spirit growing out of the war fever. "Let me," he said,

warn you in the most solemn manner against the baneful effects of the spirit of party in general.

This spirit, unfortunately, is inseparable from our nature, having its root in the strongest passions of the human mind. It exists under different shapes in all governments, more or less stifled, controlled, or repressed; but in those of the popular form it is seen in its greatest rankness and is truly their worst enemy. . . .

Against the insidious wiles of foreign influence (I conjure you to believe me, fellow citizens) the jealousy of a free people ought to be constantly awake, since history and experience prove that foreign influence is one of the most baneful foes of republican government. . . .

The great rule of conduct for us in regard to foreign nations is, in extending our commercial relations, to have with them as little political connection as possible.

A problem in Euclid could not have been more calmly and closely reasoned. Having done so, Washington went home, and left his successor to cope with the impertinence of the press.

In some ways John Adams, of Braintree, Massachusetts, second president of the United States, fared worse. Washington's two elections had been unanimous; Adams had won over Thomas Jefferson, who ran against him, by a scant margin. He became in the Republican phrase "the three-vote president." Besides, Washington had been a fine figure of a president, six feet tall and commanding in the saddle. For Adams, balding, short and pudgy, the title "his rotundity, the Duke of Braintree" was all too apt.

So mudslinging continued; meanwhile, some Americans came very near to feeling what it meant to be physically embroiled in a foreign war. These were American sailors. France and England made it a habit to seize American sailors off their ships on the Atlantic, taking them and employing them on their own vessels. Their navies were shorthanded; Jack Tar, as American sailors of the day were called, could fill the ranks and supply some muscle and brawn.

This ruthless practice of impressment has left to history some narratives by the victims. A curious one was *A narrative of Joshua Davis, who was pressed and served on board six ships of the British navy.* He was in seven engagements, once wounded, five times confined in irons, and obtained his liberty by desertion.

Davis had first sailed out of Boston on a privateer, the *Jason*, in 1779 when he was captured and pressed into the service of the British Navy. He was nineteen years old at that time, but must have been nearer thirty when he was again at liberty and employed his pen in writing his advice to other American sailors captured by warring powers at sea. A *Narrative* was a series of journal entries; Davis explained he had made them during his service, then hid them away in a sock "which I always carefully preserved . . . but not without repeated risques of losing them."

The author opened by advising peaceable submission;

was there any other alternative for an American sailor alone on the Atlantic caught aboard one of "his Britannic majesty's floating torments"? He addressed his fellow sailors:

MY FRIENDS, *after the officer has taken your name, country, sex, age, &c., down on the books, you are sent to the steward, who will then put you in a mess [eating schedule], and will tell you to go about the ship and find a messmate. Now is your time to avoid trouble. In the first place, inquire if any of your countrymen are on board, with whom you can mess. If not, endeavor to find one man (and only one) that is willing to mess with you; for as sure as you go into a mess that has either 4, 6, 8, 10, or 12 in the mess, the time will come when you will wish you had not joined them; as you may be sure of having disputes when the gin begins to operate. If they fall to fighting, endeavor to avoid taking another's part, and thereby get yourself into a scrape for if you beat one, another will challenge you; and if you chance to beat them all, it is nothing to boast of. It would be a wonder if you should come off without two black eyes, a bloody nose, your face bruised, and your ribs broken. . . .*

So steer clear of entanglements aboard His Majesty's ships, Joshua said. Besides, at sea American sailors were subject to British naval law. It was a harsh law. A sailor who stole—perhaps he stole food, sea rations were well known for being short—had to run the gauntlet, where the crew lined up in two rows on deck and you, at sword-point, walked slowly between while being whipped with "nettles," probably made of twisted and knotted ropes. Let there be no resistance.

It is in vain for you to cry, scream, jump, roll, for you must grin and bear it, as none will pity you. Finally, you will look like a piece of raw beef from your neck to the waist of your trowsers—You are taken down to the cockpit, and there have salt brine rubbed on your back, by the doctor's mate. If you should be so fortunate as to get over this, you must go to work again.

Davis had apparently observed the melancholy hanging of one of his impressed countrymen, for he wrote,

If you strike an admiral, a commodore, captain or lieutenant, you are tried by a court martial and sentenced to be hung up at the yard arm, or be flogged through the fleet. You have a right to speak in your behalf, and choose whether you will be hung or flogged. On the morning of the execution, a yellow flag is hoisted at the fore-top-masthead, as a signal, and a bow gun is fired, to inform the fleet, who lower their colors at half mast . . . the captain then comes up to the forecastle, and makes a short prayer—after which the master at arms turns to you and says, "You are to be hung by the neck under that yard, until you are dead, dead, dead; and may the Lord have mercy on your soul."

This kind of abuse at sea had been protested to France and England by the Washington Administration; so it was again by John Adams's. Then, in 1797, three commissioners, sent to negotiate these difficulties with France, received a strange reply from the French foreign minister Talleyrand. Negotiations could take place only on two conditions: a substantial loan from America, and a bribe of a quarter million dollars to the French official. This seemed an insult to the nation, though it was, if not diplomatic etiquette, quite according to the rules of the game in European diplomacy.

The Golden Vanity

This ballad was a favorite with seamen of all nations because it expressed clearly the hardship and oppression they faced.

was a lof – ty ship came from the North Coun – try, And the

2. Oh, we had a little cabin boy, and boldly up spoke he,
   And he said to the captain, "What will you give me,
   If I'll swim alongside of the Spanish enemy,
   And I sink her in the lowland, lowland low,
      If I sink her in the lowland sea?"

3. "Of gold and silver I will give you fee,
   And my only daughter your bonny bride to be,
   If you'll swim alongside of the Spanish enemy
   And you sink them in the lowland, lowland, low,
      If you sink them in the lowland sea."

4. Then the boy bared his breast and overboard sprang he,
   And he swam til he came to the Spanish enemy,
   Then with his auger sharp in her sides he bored holes three,
   And he sank her in the lowland, lowland low,
      He sank her in the lowland sea.

5. Now some were playing at cards and some were playing at
      dice,
   And some were sitting by giving very good advice,
   Until the salt water it flashed into their eyes,
   And it sank them in the lowland, lowland low,
      It sank them in the lowland sea.

6. Then the boy swam back to the cheering of the crew
   But the captain would not heed him, for his promise he did
      rue,
   And he scorned his proud entreaties, though full loudly he
      did sue,
   And he left him in the lowland, lowland low,
      He left him in the lowland sea.

7. So the boy swam round til he came to the larboard side,
   And to his messmates bitterly he cried,
   "Oh messmates pick me up, for I'm drifting with the tide,
   And I'm sinking in the lowland, lowland low,
      I'm sinking in the lowland sea."

8. Then his messmates took him up, and upon the deck he died,
   And they sewed him in his hammock, which was so large
      and wide,
   And they lowered him overboard, and he drifted with the
      tide,
   And he sank beneath the lowland, lowland low,
   He sank beneath the lowland sea.

"No, no! Not a sixpence!" cried the American negotiators at Paris, and at home this phrase was translated, "Millions for defense, not one cent for tribute." All the details were revealed through publication of the "XYZ papers," the letters being code for the names of the French negotiators. The XYZ Affair, as it was called, roused the country to a patriotic fervor and brought President Adams his one brief spurt of popularity. He got what he wanted from Congress, the beginnings of the United States Navy. He also got what he did not want at all, a "provisional army"—by which Federalist warhawks were preparing to muster against France. And he also got the Alien and Sedition Acts, the first designed to discourage foreigners, the second to muzzle the Republican press.

The Sedition Act, to remain in effect two years, provided that:

If any person shall write, print, utter or publish, or shall cause or procure to be written, printed, uttered or published . . . any false, scandalous and malicious writing or writings against the government of the United States, of either house of Congress . . . or the President . . . with intent to defame the said government . . . or to bring them into contempt or disrepute; or to excite against

*them . . . the hatred of the good people of the United
States . . . then such person, being thereof convicted before any court of the United States . . . shall be punished
by a fine not exceeding two thousand dollars, or by imprisonment not exceeding two years.*

The Alien Acts, with which this bill was associated,
were never enforced, except by temporarily raising the
residence requirement for naturalization from five to fourteen years. Some French refugees fled the country before
the act could be invoked against them. It also caused a
flurry in the South, where masters believed that the president would take advantage of the law to export their
slaves.

The Sedition Act was enforced, despite the first article
of the Bill of Rights which had read, "Congress shall
make no law . . . abridging the freedom of speech or of
the press." As the Sedition Act was being framed, however, there seemed room to argue whether it was constitutional or not. As often happens, events would decide.
Certainly there was little question in the minds of arch-
Federalists that convictions could be obtained by it; they
already had in mind their first target.

Or so they thought. He was Republican Congressman
Matthew Lyon from Fair Haven, Vermont, which he had
founded after emigration from Connecticut. Born in
Ireland, Lyon's father was believed to have been executed
by the British as one of the rebelling "white boys." Lyon
himself had come to America in his teens as a bonded servant; in Vermont, he had served in the Revolution with
Ethan Allen's Green Mountain Boys, married Allen's

niece, and on her death married the daughter of Governor Thomas Chittenden.

While the Alien and Sedition Acts were being debated by Congress Lyon had also caused a scandal, by spitting in the face of a Federalist, Roger Griswold of Connecticut, who had gone out of his way to insult him. For this unseemly conduct, Congress had tried to expel both him and later Griswold, who had attacked the "spitting Lyon" (Porcupine quickly labeled him) with a cane. Unable to get the required two-thirds majority, both attempts failed. But the incident had got full coverage in the press and inspired America's first political cartoon.

Abigail Adams, the President's wife, had kept her sister informed.

You must have heard of the spitting animal. This act so low, vulgar and base, which having been committed, could only have [been] dignifiedly resented by the expulsion of the Beast, has been spun out, made the object of party, and rendered thus the disgrace of the national legislature. . . . The circumstances were so fully proved of Lyon's being the base aggressor [having spit before he was caned], that as gentlemen, I could not have believed they could have got one third of the members to have consented to this continuance with him. . . . In the meantime the business of the nation is neglected, to the great mortification of the Federalists.

She had enclosed clippings from Porcupine's *Gazette*. This editor was, to her view, on the side of the angels, that is, the Federalists. But her sound critical sense recognized defects even in so staunch a supporter of her husband's administration: "He can write very hand-somely, and he can also descend and be as low and vulgar as a fishwoman." The enclosure represented Porcupine's fishwife aspect.

Tomorrow at 11 o'clock [it read] will be exposed to public view the Lyon of Vermont. This singular animal is said to have been caught on the bogs of Hibernia [Ireland], and when a whelp transported to America; curiosity induced a New Yorker to buy him, and moving into the country, afterwards exchanged him for a yoke of young bulls with a Vermontese.

He was petted in the neighborhood of Governor Chittenden, and soon became so domesticated that a daughter of his Excellency would stroke him and play with him as a monkey. He differs considerably from the African lion, is much more clamorous and less magnanimous. His pelt resembles more the wolf or the tiger, and his gestures bear a remarkable affinity to the bear; this, however, may be ascribed to his having been in the habit of associating with that species of wild beast on the mountain; he is carnivorous but not very ferocious—has never been detected in having attacked a man, but report says he will beat women. . . .

It will be seen in the proceedings of Congress that this beast asked leave to be excused from going with the rest of the members to wait on the President.

The last reference was to an even earlier incident, which had offended both the president and his lady. During Washington's Administration, it had been the custom of Congress to march in a body to the president to reply to his first address in person. Lyon had denounced this courtesy as a "boyish piece of business" and demanded that it be abolished. He explained it thus:

No better time could ever arrive . . . than this, which was the threshold of a new presidency, at a time when the man elected to the office was beloved and revered by his fellow citizens; he [Adams] was as yet unused to vain adulation; he had spent a great part of his life amongst a people whose love of plainness of manners forbids all pageantry; he would be glad to see the custom done away.

Adams would not have been glad at all; he was a stickler for receiving any dignity granted his predecessor. It would be left to Thomas Jefferson, when he became president, to agree with Lyon and abolish the "boyish piece of business." But that was still in the future.

Federalist members of the House had denounced Lyon's proposition and "hoped there would be enough American blood to carry the question." This remark had sent Lyon into a genealogical discussion. He said that he

had no objection to gentlemen of high blood carrying this address. He had no pretensions to high blood, though he thought he had as good blood as any of them, as he was born of a fine, hale, healthy woman. . . . He could not say, it was true, that he was descended from the bastards of [the Englishman] Oliver Cromwell or his courtiers, or from the Puritans who punished their horses for breaking the Sabbath, or from those [English] who persecuted the Quakers or hanged the witches. He could, however, say that this was his country, because he had no other, and he owned a share of it, which he had bought by means of honest industry; he had fought for his country. In every day of trouble he had repaired to her standard, and had conquered by it. Conquest had led his country to independence, and being independent he called no man's blood in question.

It was not for these remarks, which Oliver Cromwell would have judged libelous, that Lyon was jailed for sedition, almost as soon as he got to Vermont at the end of congressional session. It was not even for his publication in Vermont of *Lyon's Republican Magazine, the Scourge of Aristocracy and Repository of Political Truths,* dedicated to attacking the "high Mightinesses in our own country." It was for something far plainer, as we shall see.

Federal marshals knocked on the door of his home at Fair Haven on October 5, 1798, to prosecute him under the Sedition Act, and so he shortly went to trial. The official record of the trial has been lost. (Adams would one day be accused of somehow reaching a long hand to Vermont to suppress it.) But Lyon wrote his own account, in a letter to Republican friend in Virginia. It began:

I take the liberty to trouble you with a recital of what has happened to me, within about ten days past. On Thursday, the fifth of this month [October], I was informed that a Grand Jury had been collected to attend the Federal Court at Rutland, about 15 miles from my place of residence; . . . that the Jury was composed of men who had been accustomed to speak ill of me; that they had received a charge to look to the breaches of the

*Sedition Law; and that they had some publications of
mine under consideration.*

It looked as if the jury was going to be stacked against
him, but Lyon did not wish to evade trial. So firmly was
he convinced that the Sedition Act was unconstitutional
that when in Vermont he was urged "to be out of the
way of being taken," he welcomed instead the chance to
test the law in court. He explained,

*It could not be honorable to run away—I felt conscious
that I had done no wrong, and my enemies should never
have it to say that I ran from them.*

*An officer of the court had been in my neighborhood
the same evening to summon witnesses. I had told him
if the court wanted me, he need bring no posse, he
might come alone. I would go with him, there should be
no resistance.*

The initial charge at the trial was "scandalous and seditious utterance tending to overthrow the government,"
and "libelling the president." Lyon was asked to plead.

*I was called upon to know if I was ready, to plead to the
indictment. I answered, that I was always ready to say
I was not guilty of the charges in the indictment, but
that I was not provided with counsel, there being no
person at Rutland I was willing to trust with my own
cause.*

The first count against Lyon was of "having mali-
ciously &c. with intent &c. written at Philadelphia, a letter dated the 29th of June [1798], and published the

same at Windsor, in the newspaper called the *Vermont Journal*." The letter had been written several days before passage of the act, which was being applied retroactively, hence doubly unconstitutionally, in Lyon's case.

Into the now-missing record was read:

As to the Executive, when I shall see the efforts of that power bent on the promotion of the comfort, the happiness and accommodation of the people, the Executive shall have my zealous and uniform support; but whenever I shall, on the part of the Executive, see every consideration of public welfare swallowed up in a continual grasp for power, in an unbounded thirst for ridiculous pomp, foolish adulation, and selfish avarice; when I shall behold men of real merit daily turned out of office for no other cause but independency of sentiment; when I shall see men of firmness, merit, years, abilities and experience discarded in their applications for office for fear they possess that independence, and men of meanness preferred for the ease with which they take up and advocate opinions, the consequence of which they know but little of— when I shall see the sacred name of religion employed as a state engine to make mankind hate and persecute one another, I shall not be their humble advocate.

This was much less libelous than Porcupine's writing. Why was not the editor of *Vermont Journal* standing trial with Lyon? That editor, a Federalist, was spared the indignity, for under a Federalist administration the act was being invoked only against Republicans. (Elsewhere, a mere compositor was imprisoned for setting type for a bit of "sedition.") Whether or not the Sedition Act was in violation of the Constitution, such partiality in enforcing it certainly was.

Nonetheless, Lyon defended himself by denying that his remarks about the president's thirst for "ridiculous pomp and adulation" were libel, since they were true. Had not the judge noticed it, he inquired. Judge William Paterson said he had not.

Another of the prosecution's tactics was to convict Lyon by association—with one Joel Barlow, a Connecticut diplomat and poet who had caught the revolutionary spirit of Paris. Barlow had also written a letter, but his had mentioned "the bullying speech of your President and stupid answer of your Senate," about the French bribe; he wondered if John Adams ought not be sent "to a madhouse." Now:

The Attorney produced evidence to shew that the printed pamphlet, entitled, a Copy of a Letter from a Diplomatic Character in France, was taken from a manuscript in my hand, and the printer said he received the copy from my wife. [But] The evidence [witnesses] all agreed that I had ever been opposed to printing the letter, and gave for reason, that I had promised the gentleman, to whom the original had been written, that I would not suffer it to be printed. . . .

But apparently Lyon had read the letter aloud to a group of people at Middletown, Connecticut. Witnesses

were brought to swear they heard me read the letter, said to be the letter from a Diplomatic character in France, from a manuscript copy, supposed to be in my own handwriting; they were enquired of, Whether the reading of the letter caused any tumult? One of the evidences, a young Lawyer, and another person, an associate of his, said that they thought it did at Middletown. One of them said he heard one person say, there must be a revolution; and they both agreed that there was a noise and some tumult after the reading of that letter and some other papers.

Was he inciting the crowd? Lyon denied it. He cross-examined the witnesses, and

On enquiring of them the cause of the tumult, and their opinion, if there would have been any there, if they had not followed me on purpose to make disturbance? they acknowledged they thought if they had not been there, there would have been no disturbance. . . .

As another aspect of his defense, Lyon argued that the sedition law violated freedom of speech, but: "My plea was overruled."

As the trial drew to a close, Justice Patterson delivered his charge to the jury which Lyon described as follows:

After telling the Jury, if they leaned any way, it ought to be in favor of the defendant, he proceeded to dwell on the intention and wickedness of it, in the most elaborate manner; he descended to insinuate that the Barlow letter, as it was called, was a forgery; he said, let men of letters read that letter and compare it with Barlow's writing, and they would pronounce it none of his. He told the Jury that my defense was merely an appeal to their feelings, calculated to excite their pity; but mercy, he said, did not belong to them, that was lodged in another place, they were to follow the law, which he explained in his own way, and supported the constitutionality of it.

The jury retired about eight o'clock in the evening, and in an hour returned with a verdict: guilty. Then

The Judge, after an exodium on the nature of the offense, the malignity in me, particularly being a member of Congress, and the lenity of the Sedition Bill, which did not allow the Judges to carry the punishment so far as the common law did, pronounced sentence that I should be imprisoned four calendar months, pay a fine of 1000 dollars, and stand committed [held in custody] until the judgement should be complied with.

Lyon was alarmed by the severity of the sentence. As a member of Congress he had supposed he had immunity from imprisonment. Nor did he suppose his incarceration would be immediate, without giving him a chance to go home to settle his affairs. But now Federal Marshal Jabez Finch approached him, and

called me to him and ordered me to sit down on a certain seat in the courthouse; he called two persons to give me in charge to. I asked if they would go with me to my lodgings a few minutes, so that I might take care of my papers? I was answered in a surly manner, No, and commanded to sit down, I stood up. After the court adjourned, I enquired what was to be done with me until committment; I expected I should be confined in the prison in Rutland, the county where I lived: I was told the Marshal was authorized to imprison me in what gaol in the state he pleased, and that I must go to Vergennes, about 44 miles north of Rutland, and about the same distance from my seat at Fair Haven. I enquired what were the accommodations there? and was answered in a manner peculiar to the Marshal himself, that they were very good.

Lyon had met Jabez Finch before.

The Marshal was a man, who acted as clerk to some persons whom I had occasion to transact some business with, about a dozen years since; when he first came into this country, in which he behaved so, that I have ever since most heartily despised him; this he has no doubt seen and felt.

The dislike between the two would make Lyon's imprisonment harder, as it would the two-day horseback ride to jail at Vergennes. Lyon had assured Finch he would travel there willingly, but the marshal

said he would not trust to that and prepared two troopers, with their pistols to guard me. . . .

On Wednesday evening last I was locked up in this room, where I now am; it is about sixteen feet long by twelve wide, with a necessary [toilet facilities] in one corner, which affords a stench about equal to the Philadelphia docks in the month of August.

This cell is the common receptacle for horsethieves, moneymakers, runaway Negroes, or any kind of felon. There is a half-moon through the door, sufficient to receive a plate through and for my friends to look through and speak to me. There is a window placed on the opposite side, about twenty inches by sixteen, crossed by nine square iron bars to keep the cold out; consequently I have to walk smartly with my great coat on to keep comfortably warm some mornings.

At first Lyon was virtually incommunicado in jail; pen and ink were

offered me; but the Gaoler said, it was against his orders, I must not have it. The marshal paid me a visit on Thursday evening; he examined the cell, looked on my little table, to see what was there; but he found nothing. . . . I enquired of him, then or before, what situation I was to consider myself in, with regard to the use of pen and ink? His answer was, I might use them, but he must see everything I sent out of the gaol; if I conducted myself otherwise (looking at a chain that lay on the floor) he said he would put me in a situation that I could not write.

I asked him what he meant by that? He told me, I was at his disposal, and if I did not behave like a prisoner, he would send me to Woodstock gaol.—I told him there would be one advantage in that, he would not be there always, and I should get rid of the sight of him.

So frequently history is played out on a most human scale; the next episode reads like *The Count of Monte Cristo*.

I observed a man hammering on the prison door. You seem much concerned about that door (said I) there has scarce been an hour since I came here, but there has been some person hammering at the door, or putting new bolts and bars. It is all useless, said I; if I wished to come out, they could not hold me; and as I do not, if my limits were marked by a single thread, I would not overstep it. He replied, he was only nailing up an advertisement. Next morning when the house was very still I heard some person step up and read the advertisement on the door.

The person must have read it aloud, for Lyon learned

it contained a preamble concerning my having complained that I was debarred the use of pen, ink, and paper, and a declaration that I had leave to furnish myself with those things, and use them as I thought proper, signed by the Marshal. . . .

I, next morning, sent for a number of friends, who got admittance, and after some conversation on the subject, before the gaoler, and getting his explanation of the advertisement, that he considered me now allowed to write, without submitting my productions to the Marshal.

Not censored, Lyon had begun his long letter to his Republican friend:

I was solemnly invested with pen and ink. The first use I have made of it, after a line to my wife, is to write you this long prolix account of the fruits of this beloved Sedition bill. You may remember that I told you, when it was passing, that it was doubtless intended for members of Congress, and very likely would be brought to bear on me the very first; so it has happened.

While Lyon was in jail he was reelected to Congress by a large majority. For his imprisonment he and his Republican friends blamed John Adams. This was unfair. What Adams called the "half war" with France ended in 1799 when the president responded to French peace feelers; and the war fever that lay in back of the passage of the Sedition Act collapsed.

The following year Adams and his administration moved to Washington, D.C. Setting up the new national capital had taken the better part of ten years. An Act of Congress passed in 1790 decreed that the seat of the federal government would be set amid the forests that bordered the Potomac. So the trees began to be cleared, and the city to be laid out with broad avenues radiating from the site of the Capitol, like spokes from the hub of the wheel.

But the years passed and the work of building proceeded very slowly. Washington in 1800 was a dreary place. As the president's wife, Abigail Adams, described it, "a new country, with houses scattered over a space of ten miles, and trees and stumps in plenty." As for the White House, only one wing was finished, and a damp and dismal shell it was. "Not one room or chamber," Abigail complained to her sister Mary, "is finished. . . . It is habitable by fires in every part, thirteen of which we are obliged to keep daily, or sleep in wet and damp places."

As for the halls of Congress, they were not even as far along as the White House, and there was hardly any place for congressmen to live. As Secretary of the Treasury Oliver Wolcott, said, "I don't see how members of Congress can possibly secure lodgings unless they will consent to live like scholars in a college, or monks in a monastery, ten or twenty crowded in one house."

For Abigail and her husband, living in the damp and expensive White House was tribulation enough. Worse was to come when the Jeffersonians won the elections of 1800. To the Adamses this seemed a catastrophe almost as terrible as the end of the world. "If ever," lamented Abigail, "we saw a day of darkness, I fear this is the one which will be visible until kindled into flames."

It had taken prolonged balloting to elect Jefferson over his opponent, Aaron Burr—by exactly one vote. That vote, his friends would always claim, was cast by the Lyon of Vermont.

CONCLUSION

The period in American history that followed the Revolution, and that ended with Thomas Jefferson's election to the presidency in 1801, was stamped with a special significance all its own. The country emerged from the dislocation of war under the leadership of the Federalists, the same party that had led the revolutionary struggle itself. The Federalists created a new Constitution, secured its ratification by the nation, and began the work of setting up and organizing a central government endowed with real, not just theoretical, power. A beginning was made, through the instrumentality of the Northwest Ordinance, in organizing the fertile lands that had been won by conquest from Great Britain.

These were impressive achievements, but the story reveals, too, that bitter struggles underlay them; that there were rifts in American society which, growing deeper with the passage of time, have endured to this very day. Farmers and pioneers showed a deep fear and distrust of governmental power which, they were convinced, was more likely to be used to defeat their interests than to protect them. Two rebellions, one in Massachusetts and the other in Pennsylvania, underlined the fact that these fears were not imaginary nightmares, but were based on social realities.

These same farmers and pioneers had given constitutional expression to their feelings by insisting on a bill of rights that would define the power of government, and set eternal limits to this power. But the Bill of Rights did more than this, as the farmers' rebellions proved. It provided guidelines for the people in their future struggles against oppressive government—struggles which, as so many of the people realized, were bound to come.

Yet another rift was clear in 1790, but its depth had not yet been probed—the rift created by the institution of slavery. At the end of the Revolutionary War the future of American slavery was in doubt: the war had witnessed the beginnings of a movement of liberation that would lead, some years before the Civil War, to the emancipation of almost all the slaves that had been held in the North.

But the South was where most of the nation's 800,000 slaves were, and there the issue remained in doubt throughout the Federalist era. After the turn of the century these slaves would be dragged out to the West in increasing numbers; they would be set to work growing cotton and tobacco on the broad lands south of the Ohio River.

This rift, in other words, was going to grow with time, not lessen. It underlined the incompleteness of the American Revolution. On its banners the Revolution had inscribed the rights of man—of all men. But for a black man there would not be any rights that a white man was bound to respect. Out of this fact would one day come new and bloody struggles for human freedom, the end of which is not yet.

The struggles that ordinary people waged with their government involved not only questions of taxation, debts, and the right to freedom: they involved the question of war and peace. An object lesson in the dangers of governmental tyranny came with the passage of the Sedition Act in 1798; this was a legal tool of the Federalists to silence popular opposition to an unwelcome war with France. With Jefferson's electoral victory in 1800 this law was allowed to lapse; but it lay around for more than a century like an unexploded bomb. In 1917 another federal government picked it up, dusted it off, and passed it once more into law to silence American opposition to what many considered the odious intervention in World War I. Yet another administration found the Sedition Act a handy tool, in the form of the Smith Act of 1940, to squelch opposition to American involvement in World War II.

The life of the ordinary man in the early Republic was a hard one. Hours of labor were long and incessant, and the daily life of factory and frontier was often dangerous. Women, too, had little rest from their daily chores; they grew old before their time and lost the bloom of youth in rearing large families and in the daily battle for survival. To an extent that is sometimes hard for us to realize, these people lived in the constant shadow of death and disease. The Philadelphia plague of 1793 was only one among many epidemics that were forever sweeping over the countryside, wiping out families, filling the cemeteries with tiny graves, and leaving the air loud with the tearful laments of the survivors.

SONG NOTES

All guitar arrangements copyright by John Anthony Scott.

Katie Kruel
Fairly slow (andante). "Katie Kruel" is from colonial New England. Militiamen used it as a marching song; children sang it as a jingle and speeded up the tempo; for women it was either lullaby or lament.

The Two Sisters
With deliberate speed (moderato). This song is #10 in Francis J. Child's great collection of English and Scottish ballads, and dates back hundreds of years in British and Scandinavian tradition. In Virginia it was a favorite of white and black people alike.

The Cherry Tree Carol
With deliberate speed (moderato). This beautiful medieval carol is #54 in the Child collection. It seems to have been especially popular in the Appalachian region and Virginia.

To the West
Fairly fast (allegro). The melody is a New England variant of an old English song, "The Bonny Boy."

The Banks of the Ohio
Allegro. This is a fairly common type of murder ballad, and originated in Virginia or the Northwest Territory early in the 19th century.

My Fancy Flies Free (Die Gedanken Sind Frei)
Allegro. This is a German drinking song, and an ode to freedom, hundreds of years old. It was brought to Pennsylvania by German immigrants in the 18th century, and may be considered an apt expression of the spirit and inner meaning of the Bill of Rights. The translation is by John Anthony Scott.

Cold Blows the Wind
Andante. This ballad, #78 in the Child collection, is considered by many to be one of the most exquisite laments in the English language. The melody comes from the west of England.

The Devil Came Fiddling Through the Town
Allegro. This song, by the Scots poet Robert Burns, was first published in 1792 and soon became popular in the United States.

The Golden Vanity
Moderato. One of the most famous of the old English ballads (#286 in the Child collection), "The Golden Vanity" probably dates back to the 16th century. It was a favorite with seamen on both sides of the Atlantic because it expressed so clearly the special kind of oppression which was their lot.

BIBLIOGRAPHY

General

For the history of the United States 1783–87 see Merrill Jensen. *A History of the United States during the Confederation* (New York: Random House, 1950; Vintage paperback). John C. Miller, *The Federalist Era* (New York: Harper and Co., 1960; Harper Torchbook) covers the period 1789–1801. Claude G. Bowers, *Jefferson and Hamilton: The Struggle for Democracy in America* (Boston, 1925; reissued as a Sentry paperback, Boston: Houghton Mifflin, 1966) is a readable account of the conflicts in national politics during the 1790's. For more detail see Stephen G. Kurtz, *The Presidency of John Adams* (Philadelphia: University of Pennsylvania Press, 1957; A. S. Barnes paperback) and Noble E. Cunningham, *The Jeffersonian Republicans, 1789–1801* (Chapel Hill: University of North Carolina Press, 1957). There are many studies of state life and politics during the period; special mention may be made of Richard J. Purcell, *Connecticut in Transition: 1775–1818* (Middletown: Wesleyan University Press, 1963; a new edition of a work published originally in 1918).

For the foreign policy of this period perhaps the best introduction is Felix Gilbert, *To the Farewell Address: Ideas of Early American Foreign Policy* (Princeton, N.J.: Princeton University Press, 1961). Samuel Flagg Bemis' detailed works on Pinckney's and Jay's Treaties are available in paperback editions (New Haven: Yale University Press, 1960 and 1962 respectively).

Alexander Hamilton's famous *Reports* are available in paperback (New York: Harper and Row, 1964: Harper Torchbook), ed. Jacob E. Cooke. Jefferson, Hamilton and John Adams papers are available in multivolume editions .sued respectively by Princeton, Columbia, and Harvard University Presses.

A Young Heir

There are a number of excellent accounts of the United States at the end of the Revolutionary War by foreign observers, notably Johann David Schoepf, *Travels in the Confederation, 1783–4* (1911: reissued New York: Franklin, Burt, 1968); and Marquis de Chastellux, *Travels in North America in the Years 1780, 1781 and 1782* (1786: reissued Chapel Hill, N.C.: University of North Carolina Press, 1963. Translated and edited by Howard C. Rise, Jr.). Joseph Plumb Martin's *Narrative* is available under the title *Private Yankee Doodle, Being a Narrative of Some of the Dangers, Adventures, and Sufferings of a Revolutionary Soldier* (Boston: Little, Brown and Co., 1962. New York: Popular Library paperback, 1963. Ed. George F. Scheer).

A Flawed Freedom

Jefferson's own writings and journals were the basis for this chapter. See in particular his *Notes on the State of Virginia* (Chapel Hill, N.C.: University of North Carolina Press, 1955; Harper Torchbook. Ed. William Peden); and the fascinating *Farm Book* (Charlottesville, Va.: University of Virginia, 1953. Ed. Edwin Betts. Reissued by the American Philosophic Society). See also Duc de La Rochefoucault-Liancourt, *Travels Through the United States* (1800. Reissued by Kelley Publishers, Clifton, N.J.: 1972, 4 vols.)

To the West

Samuel Forman, *Narrative of a Journey Down the Ohio and Mississippi in 1790*, and Timothy Flint, *Indian Wars of the West* have been reissued by Arno Press (New York: 1971 and 1971 respectively). The text of the Northwest Ordinance is available in a paperback, *Living Documents in American History* vol. I (New York: Washington Square Press, 1964. Ed. John Anthony Scott).

The Commotions in Massachusetts
A standard source for the Shays' rebellion in G. R. Minot *History of the Insurrection in Massachusetts in 1786* (1788. Reissued New York: Plenum Press, 1971). Marion Starkey, *A Little Rebellion* (New York: Alfred A. Knopf, 1955) is out of print.

The Constitutional Convention and the Bill of Rights
The fundamental source materials for a study of the Constitutional Convention were published under the editorship of Max Farrand in 1911. This important work is available in a 4-volume paperback edition: *The Records of the Federal Convention of 1787* (New Haven: Yale University Press, 1966). The most important commentary on the Constitution is the collection of *Federalist Papers* put together by Alexander Hamilton, James Madison and John Jay. This work is available in an excellent paperback edition edited by Clinton Rossiter (New York: Mentor Books, 1961).

The Federalist Papers were produced as a contribution to the great debate over ratification of the Constitution. For the anti-Federalist viewpoint in this debate see Cecelia M. Kenyon ed. *The Antifederalists* (New York: Bobbs-Merrill, 1966; American Heritage series paperback), and Jackson T. Main, *The Antifederalists* (Raleigh, N.C.: University of North Carolina Press, 1961; Quadrangle paperback). The ratification debates at the State level are reproduced in Jonathan Elliot ed., *Debates in the Several State Conventions* (1836. Reissued New York: Franklin, Burt, 1968). Other contemporary commentary is reproduced by Paul L. Ford ed. *Essays on the Constitution of the United States 1787–8* (1892. Reissued New York: Franklin, Burt, 1967).

Various monographs are available concerning the struggle over ratification, notably: Samuel B. Harding, *The Contest Over* the Ratification of the Federal Constitution in the State of *Massachusetts* (New York: DaCapo Press, 1969); Ernest W. Spaulding, *New York in the Critical Period 1783–89* (1932. Reissued Port Washington: Ira J. Friedman, 1963); and John McMaster and F. B. Stone, *Pennsylvania and the Federal Constitution 1787–8* (New York: DaCapo Press, 1969).

Charles Beard's pioneer study *An Economic Interpretation of the Constitution of the U.S.A.* (1913) is available as a Macmillan paperback. See also Robert E. Brown, *Charles Beard and the Constitution: A Critical Analysis of an Economic Interpretation of the Constitution* (Princeton: University of Princeton Press, 1956. Norton paperback, 1965.) For the story of the Bill of Rights and its incorporation into the Constitution, see Robert A. Rutland, *Birth of the Bill of Rights 1776–91* (New York: Macmillan, 1955; Collier paperback).

The Philadelphia Plague
For a general account of the pestilence in Philadelphia see J. H. Powell, *Bring Out Your Dead* (Philadelphia: University of Pennsylvania Press, 1949; reissued by Arno Press, 1970), and for the biography of Benjamin Rush, Carl Binger, *Revolutionary Doctor: Benjamin Rush 1746–1813* (New York: W. W. Norton and Co., 1966). The background for colonial medicine is provided in Richard H. Shryock, *Medicine and Society in America 1660–1860* (New York: New York University Press, 1960; Cornell University Press paperback).

The Whisky Rebellion
For western Pennsylvania in the 1790's see J. E. Wright and D. S. Corbett's charming *Pioneer Life in Western Pennsylvania* (Pittsburgh: University of Pittsburgh Press, 1968; Pitt paperback) and Solon J. and Elizabeth Buck, *The Planting of Civilization in Western Pennsylvania* (same publisher, hardcover and paperback, 1969). Leland D. Baldwin, *The Whiskey Rebels* (Pittsburgh: University of Pittsburgh Press, 1939; Pitt paperback) gives a detailed account of the uprising. Henry M. Bracken-

ridge, *History of the Western Insurrection* (1859) is an account by the son of one of the leaders (New York: Arno Press, 1969).

The Lyon of Vermont
The most recent study of the Alien and Sedition laws is James Morton Smith, *Freedom's Fetters: The Alien and Sedition Laws and American Civil Liberties* (Ithaca: Cornell University Press, 1956, and Cornell paperback, 1966). Leonard W. Levy, *Freedom of Speech and Press in Early American History: Legacy of Suppression* (New York: Harper Torchbook, 1963) places the Sedition Law in the wider context of the history of the struggle for freedom of expression.

This bibliography has been designed for the reference of teachers, students, and school librarians. All works listed are in print at the time of writing (1971) unless otherwise stated.

INDEX

Singletarry, "Daddy," 166, 173; quoted, 167
Slavery, Negro, 3, 4, 32, 35, 36, 39, 47, 49, 50, 53, 56, 64, 83, 145–152 *passim*, 278
Smith, Bagwell, 53, 55, 58, 60, 63, 64
Smith, George, 53, 55, 56, 58, 60, 64
Smith, Isaac, 52–62 *passim*, 64, 146; quoted, 56, 57, 58, 59, 60
Smith, Melancthon, 170; quoted, 170, 172
Smith, Ursula, 53, 57, 58, 59, 60, 64, 68
South Carolina, 16, 32, 69, 145, 146, 148,: 150, 151, 152, 161, 163
Springfield, Mass., 120, 121, 129, 130, 131
Spy (newspaper), 105, 106, 109, 110, 113
Supreme Court, U.S., 160
Susquehanna River, 22, 232, 233–234

Talleyrand, 257
Thomas, Isaiah, 105, 106, 110, 112, 122, 126, 127, 133; quoted, 128–129
Thomas's Farmer's Almanack, 109
Thompson, General, quoted, 164–165
"To the West," song, 100–101
Tories, 22, 32, 69
Travels . . . (Schoepf), 16
"Two Sisters, The," song, 40–46

Valley Forge, 8, 21
Vermont, 24, 262, 266, 267
Vermont Journal, 268
Virginia, 16, 20, 26, 29, 31, 35, 39, 52, 53, 57, 71, 146, 150, 151, 152, 157, 173, 174, 216, 231; U.S. Constitution ratified by, 181–182

Washington, D.C., 3, 275,
Washington, George, 6, 8, 13, 14, 16, 33, 34, 38, 53, 59, 134, 135, 136, 147, 164, 165, 182, 184, 212, 224, 225, 228, 229, 250, 251, 254; farewell address of, 254; quoted, 33, 34, 134, 254; and Whisky Rebellion, 231, 235, 238, 239, 241, 245
Westmoreland County, Pa., 22, 85, 216, 217, 219, 224
Wharfield, Priscilla, 113, 125
Wheatley, Phillis, 49
Wheeler, Glazier, 112, 125
Whisky Boys, 226–227, 235, 242
Whisky Rebellion, 5, 231–235, 237–239, 241–247
White House, 275, 276
Whiting, William, 162
Widgery, William, 163
Williamsburg, Va., 26, 57
Wilson, James, 144
Wolcott, Oliver, 275
Woodbridge, Joshua, quoted, 129–130
Worcester, Mass., 103, 105, 110, 128, 130
Worcester Magazine, 113, 116, 117, 122, 125, 126, 128, 129, 131, 133
Wyoming Valley, 22

XYZ Affair, 261

Yeomen of Massachusetts, 165
Yorktown, Va., 26, 28, 57, 58

MARION STARKEY is a well-known historian and specialist on the Federalist period. She is the author of many books, among them *The Cherokee Nation*, *The Devil in Massachusetts*, and *A Little Rebellion*, which is a detailed study of Shays' uprising of 1786.

A graduate of Boston University, and the recipient of two Guggenheim fellowships, Miss Starkey has also worked as a newspaper editor and book reviewer, and has taught at the University of Connecticut and Hampton Institute in Virginia. She lives in Saugus, Massachusetts.

JOHN ANTHONY SCOTT has taught at Columbia and Amherst colleges, and since 1951 has been Chairman of the Department of History at the Fieldston School, New York. He is currently Professor of Legal History at Rutgers University. Among the numerous books he has authored or edited are *The Ballad of America*, *The Diary of the American Revolution*, and *Trumpet of Prophecy*.

Text set in Electra
Printed and bound by Jenkins-Universal Corporation, N.Y., N.Y.
Series styled by Atha Tehon
This book was designed by Barbara Bert